When Pigs Fly!

Training Success With Impossible Dogs

Jane Killion

Wenatchee, Washington U.S.A.

When Pigs Fly! Training Success With Impossible Dogs
Jane Killion

Dogwise Publishing
A Division of Direct Book Service, Inc.
403 South Mission Street, Wenatchee, Washington 98801
1-509-663-9115, 1-800-776-2665
www.dogwisepublishing.com / info@dogwisepublishing.com
© 2007 Jane Killion

Graphic Design: Nathan Woodward
Cover Photo: Louis B. Ruediger
Indexing: Cheryl Smith
Photographs: Louis B. Ruediger

Dogwise Publishing would like to give a special thanks to Lou for all of the amazing photos and hard work he has put into this book.

Cataloging-in-Publication Data is available upon request from the Library of Congress
Library of Congress Control Number: 2007011652
ISBN: 1-929242-44-1
Printed in the U.S.A.

Table of Contents

For Nicky

Introduction

If you are reading this, you probably have not had much success with training your dog. You might even think of your dog as an "impossible" dog to train. Despite your bribing, begging, and threatening him, he still ignores you and carries on his merry way, often leaving a path of destruction in his wake. He is a charismatic character and a fine companion, but he does not care a fig about what you want him to do. He is a dog with an agenda and if you don't fit into that agenda, so much the worse for you.

Are you mad to own a dog like that? Unlike you, your friends have nice dogs that sit by their side, quietly awaiting their masters' next command. They are mild mannered dogs who would never dream of dismembering the couch. They come immediately every time their owner calls them. They do useful tricks, like fetching the paper, at their masters' bidding. They are no trouble, at all.

Despite the fact that your dog presents some challenges, there is nothing wrong with your dog and nothing wrong with you for owning him. If goodness and obedience were the only criteria we used to pick out friends and mates, there would be powerful few marriages or friendships. If over-achievers were the only people that ever got dates, we would almost all be sitting home Friday nights. If instant compliance with any rule we set were the only thing we cared about in children, the majority of children would be completely unloved.

Fortunately, we don't limit our affection to people who are good, obedient, workaholics. I would prefer to be around someone who is fabulous than someone who is good, and that feeling extends to dogs as well as people. This book is dedicated to making it possible to live happily with a dog who is fabulous, but not particularly "good." Welcome to the world where your dog can be trained to behave just as well as any other dog—When Pigs Fly.

1

The Impossible Dream

Your Dog Can be Trained!

Are you having trouble getting your dog to do even the most basic things, like sit, come when called, or walk next to you without pulling on the leash? Have you been to obedience class and been humiliated by how inattentive and wild your dog was? Have you had to endure the accusatory looks of horror people give you as they recoil from your unruly pet? Think your dog is beyond hope? Think he is impossible to train? Get ready, because your life is about to change for the better.

Any healthy dog can be trained, and I am going to show you how to do it. By the time you finish this book your dog will be well trained, but that's not all. You and your dog will have learned to love training, and you will be training your dog whenever you get the chance, just for the fun of it. You will have the confidence that you can teach your dog anything and the understanding that your dog is capable of learning, and loving it. You and your dog will be a successful team and you will be

Walks are no fun when your dog has a mind of his own and you have no way to get him to pay attention to you.

able to live in harmony together. As improbable as this may seem to you now, this is the book where the impossible becomes possible—Pigs Can Fly!

Sound Familiar?

Three Dogs

Consider the following descriptions of three successful performance dogs. Do any of them resemble your dog?

Dog number one is "The Bolter." She attends basic obedience class. With one leash correction, she slows down. If the correction is repeated, she stops. If a third try is hazarded, she sits down like a mule and patently refuses to move. When off leash, however, this dog has no trouble moving very rapidly. Unfortunately, she is generally moving very rapidly in the wrong direction. She does not give a rat's behind about what her handler wants her to do. It takes a great deal of sweaty and frustrating effort just to capture her after she runs off. Sometimes she actually has to be tackled.

Cherry's original mission in life was to run away from me, but she eventually learned to jump through hoops for me instead!

Dog number two is "The Maniac." He is so highly excitable that his heart literally beats out of control when he is in public. He has to be on beta-blocker medication to (in the words of his vet) "keep him from keeling over." Even a walk down the street is out of the question. Anytime he meets a strange person or dogs his heart races, his tongue turns black, and he collapses on the ground. Sometimes his excitement is so great that he vomits and loses control of his bowels. One time he became so over stimulated by a visit from a neighbor that veterinary intervention was required to save his life.

Dog number three is "The Dud." She carefully and precisely follows her handler around—at a walk. Toys, food, praise, and handler gyrations bring absolutely no change in her pace. She has two speeds—dead slow or stopped.

After reading these descriptions, you may find yourself re-reading my first sentence. "Did she say successful performance dogs?" Yes, I did. These are my Bull Terriers, and they all have gone on to great performance careers.

"The Bolter" is Cherry. Shortly after I figured out how to train her, she achieved 9 agility titles, with 24 first place finishes. To get these titles, Cherry had to run off leash in an unfenced ring with hundreds of people and dogs standing nearby. She had to navigate a course of obstacles like jumps, tunnels, see saws, and a five and a half foot high A-frame, all off leash, at top speed, at my direction, without me touching her. Not bad for a dog that previously spent most of her time figuring out how to run away from me.

"The Maniac" is Nicky, who earned his first leg toward an American Kennel Club obedience title at the Bull Terrier Club of America's National Specialty, going High in Trial. To achieve this honor, Nicky had to walk exactly by my left side, turn with me, speed up and slow down with me, sit automatically when I halted, and stand still and allow the judge to run her hands down his back, both on and off leash. All of this had to be performed with little or no verbal cues from me. In addition, he had to stay in a line up of strange dogs with me 35 feet away from him for a total of five minutes. He had to perform in the hustle bustle of an obedience trial, with lots of strange dogs and people milling around. That's a long way from a dog who could not even go out on a leash walk in the neighborhood for fear of dropping dead from the excitement.

Nicky (on right) could not relax enough to go out for a walk, but now he can enjoy a stroll with some friends.

"The Dud" is Ruby who, at eighteen months, completed three agility titles. Agility requires the dog to run fast, and Ruby was as much as 10 seconds under the allowed time. Oh, by the way, she was also Winners Bitch at The Bull Terrier Club of America National Specialty that month. In order to beat out the other dogs she had to show like a house on fire for about two hours, and she did. I'd say these are remarkable accomplishments for a dog that would almost never break out of a walk.

So, what's the point?

You may or may not have interest in doing performance sports with your dog, but the fact that I could train my dogs to these advanced levels is proof that you can train yours to do any basic thing that you would like him to do. Your dog, no

Ruby, who almost never broke out of a walk when she was a young dog, now tears through agility weave poles. With the right training, Ruby went from "Dud" to "Dynamic!"

matter what his breed or type, loves to learn, and that is what this book is all about. I have never met a dog that did not like training and learning new things. Pick the dog you love first, and I will show you how to have lots of fun training him. I will give you the skills you need to shape your pal into a happy, fun companion who is a pleasure to live with. You will have a system that you can use to build the skills necessary for virtually any activity you wish to participate in with your dog. Maybe you just love your dog and wish you could teach him a few things so life would be more harmonious around the house or out on walks. Maybe you have an "odd" breed of dog and you want to earn your breed club's versatility award. Maybe you have a breed of dog that is not normally seen in performance sports and you want to get in on some of the fun your friends with obedient Shelties are having. Whatever your ultimate goal is, this book is dedicated to teaching you how to have a great time getting there.

Are you thinking, "Yeah, but my dog is too hard to train?" I sympathize with people who insist that their dog is too difficult, too stubborn, too slow, or too hyper to train, but I can't agree with them. As you can see from the stories of my own dogs, I have faced and dealt with all of those issues. The only problem that I see is that most people need a better understanding of how dogs learn and how to teach them.

Why Does My Dog Seem Hard to Train?
The Nature of the Pigs Fly Kinda Dog

Let's talk about the term "difficult to train." When we say a dog is difficult to train, part of what we really mean is that the dog is not **biddable**. Biddable means willing to do your bidding, just because you ask. Biddability is something that has been selectively bred into certain breeds that need to work closely with humans. Herding breeds need to respond to the shepherd's commands. Gun dogs need to work as a team with the hunter. Terriers need to think on their own to outsmart and kill vermin…hmm. Sounds like we bred independent thinking instead of biddability into that group.

Pig-tionary

Biddable: willing to carry out the wishes of others: amenable, compliant, conformable, docile, obedient, submissive, supple, tractable (Roget's II: The New Thesaurus, Third Edition 1995). These are qualities that have been highly prized by breeders of working dogs throughout the centuries. Careful breeding over thousands of years has cultivated dogs that have an inclination to both work with and take direction from man. If you are reading this book, you probably do not have one of those dogs. If you laughed when you read the definition of biddable you definitely do not have one of those dogs.

Before you throw up your hands and say, "Well, there it is. My dog is genetically programmed to ignore me," consider this: If you were comfortably at home watching TV, and your spouse said, "Go upstairs and pack your suitcase," you would probably say "Why?" If he or she answered, "Because I say so," you might or might not actually pack your bag, and you would probably be a little resentful about being ordered around that way. Most people would want the courtesy of an explanation. Even if you did pack your bag, you would do so reluctantly. If, instead of, "Because I say so," he or she said, "We just won the lottery and to celebrate we are going to the French Rivera!" you'd run upstairs right away and pack, wouldn't you? Well, non-biddable dogs think the same way that you do. Biddable dogs would not ask "Why?" if they were told to go upstairs and pack their bags, but non-biddable dogs would need more information before they made their choices about whether or not to comply with your request. Biddability, then, can be defined as removing the "Why?" from the dog's psyche. The biddable dog never asks why, he just does what you are asking.

So, is it such a big deal if we just have to answer the question "Why?" Why should he sit/stay/walk on loose leash, etc? Because you are his master and he is within your dominion and that was the way it went on *Lassie*? Dream on. Because you are capable of giving him the doggie equivalent of a trip to the French Rivera if he does what you want? Now, you're talkin'.

Although lack of biddability is part of what makes your dog different from "easy" breeds, there is more to it than that. Your dog is the dog who asks the questions. He acts like he is deaf when you call him, but he could figure out how to escape from a high security penitentiary if there was something he wanted on the outside. He's probably inquisitive and on fire to explore the world—always scheming, but never scheming to figure out what you want. While he appears to have no interest in doing anything you want him to do, he is almost obsessive about performing tasks of his own choosing, like chasing squirrels, sniffing, or tearing apart upholstered furniture. Although he is affectionate, his agenda does not include doing anything to please you. Far from seeking your approval, at times it seems as if he revels in the chaos that his disruptive behavior creates—sometimes you have a sneaking suspicion that he thinks it's funny when you get angry.

How do you describe a dog like that in one word or phrase? Independent? Stubborn? Hard to Train? Challenging? Obsessive? Stupid? Intelligent? These are all value-laden terms that pass judgment on the dog, his attributes, and what he should or should not be able to do. They invite us to draw negative conclusions about the dog because of a lack of understanding of dogs and how they think. I don't believe that using those kinds of words or phrases to describe your dog will further your goal of becoming a happy team with your canine companion. In this book you will find that I frequently use the term "Pigs Fly dog" as shorthand for a dog with all of the fabulous (yes, fabulous) qualities I described above. I like "Pigs Fly" because, although these dogs sometimes seem impossible to deal with, in fact they are trainable, even brilliantly trainable. I also use the term non-biddable because, although it is a more limited term, it is an accurate description of the nature of these dogs and cuts to the core of why people have trouble training them. Sometimes I will even use the terms "difficult to train," "hard to train," and the like, but they should be taken with a grain of salt. As you will see in this book, the number one rule for success is to pick out your dog's strengths and work them to your advantage. I think it is important you think of your dog in terms of all of his wonderful attributes, and not get caught up in any pre-judgment about what he can or can't do. Taking away negative labels and the stigma that goes with them is the first step in opening your mind to the potential in your dog.

Any kind of dog may fall under the Pigs Fly umbrella—purebreds and mixed breeds alike. When I talk about "Terriers" or any other breed or group of dog, it is just shorthand for a dog that shares those characteristics, mixed or purebred, with or without papers. Most of the Terrier and Hound groups can be classified as Pigs Fly dogs, but there are plenty of other breeds/mixes that can be Pigs Fly dogs, too. Generally, any dog whose original purpose was to perform a task independently, without taking direction from, or being in cooperation with, a human teammate is going to be a Pigs Fly kinda dog. If you are in doubt as to your dog's heritage, but you can't seem to get him to go along with your plans, he is in the Pigs Fly club.

A well-trained dog makes a wonderful companion.

I spend a lot of time mentoring new Bull Terrier owners. Time and time again, I hear stories about the frustration and discouragement they experience when they go to training classes with their dog. Seems like a lot of instructors don't want to be bothered with dogs that are not "easy" to train. Some instructors flat out recommend getting another breed. To me, this is just terrible. My dogs had three very different types of problems, but we worked through them, and the joy that I get every time we train or compete is beyond measure. The real reward for me was achieving things and having fun with the dogs that I already loved. I want to make that reward available to anyone who desires it. Far from wanting an "easy" dog, I love my busy terriers whose brains are turning so fast that you can hear the whirling and clicking. I make no apologies for owning a fabulous little dog that is always on the go and obsessed with living life to the hilt, and you should not be making any apologies, either. There is a gold mine of possibilities waiting inside of your Pigs Fly kinda dog and I am going to show you how to find it.

Relative "Intelligence" of Breeds
The Learning Curve is not Straightforward

One of the most fascinating books you can ever read is the American Kennel Club's *The Complete Dog Book* (New York: Ballantine Books, 2006). It contains brief descriptions and histories for the breeds of dog recognized by the AKC and one has to be amazed at how we have bred so many breeds of dogs for so many specialized tasks. There are dogs that herd livestock by driving them from behind, and there are dogs that tend livestock by heading them off. There are dogs who will go and fetch a bird without putting a single mark on it, and there are dogs that will destroy any small animal they can find. There are dogs who will diligently and quietly point out where birds are hiding, and there are dogs who will do a crazy dance to draw curious birds within gun range. There are dogs who will guard and let no one near their family (be that family human, dog, or sheep) and dogs who willingly accept handling from anyone.

Sit down, because this is going to come as a shock to you. *No breed of dog is inherently better at learning than any other breed or mix of breeds.* That's right—despite all the flashy behavior that certain breeds offer, despite the fact that some breeds of dogs are literally waiting around for you to tell them what to do, they are no quicker to learn than any other dog. That is not just my opinion—Scott and Fuller in their seminal work *Genetics and the Social Behavior of the Dog* (Chicago: University of Chicago Press, 1965) did extensive experiments with Basenjis, Shetland Sheepdogs, Beagles, Cocker Spaniels, Wire-Haired Fox Terriers, and all manner of crosses of those breeds. The tests consisted of various complicated combinations of obstacles and mazes that the dogs had to negotiate in order to get to a food reward. Scott and Fuller found that, when it came to problem solving and learning, no breed or cross of breed is quicker to learn than any other is. In their words:

> … (A)ll breeds show about the same average level of performance in problem solving, provided they can be adequately motivated, provided physical differences and handicaps do not affect the tests, and provided interfering emotional reactions such as fear can be eliminated. In short, all the breeds appear quite similar in pure intelligence.

Wait, it gets better. I am going to go out on a limb and guess that people consider a Basenji to be one of the hardest to train dogs, and a Sheltie to be one of the easiest. If you attend obedience or agility trials, you will see lots and lots of Shelties, and powerful few Basenjis. Some people will attribute this to superior intelligence and learning ability on the part of the Sheltie. Here is what Scott and Fuller found:

> In general, the four hunting breeds (beagles, basenjis, terriers, and cockers) performed best on the tests. This is probably because most of the tests were deliberately designed to test independent capacities motivated by food rewards…By contrast, the Shetland sheep dogs, whose ancestors have been selected for their ability to perform complex tasks under close direction from their human masters, performed rather badly. *Indeed, in many of the tests, the shelties gave the subjective impression of waiting around for someone to tell them what to do.* (Emphasis added)

The Basenji learned faster than the Sheltie. The Sheltie was waiting to be told what to do, and the Basenji was out there figuring it out on his own. So, if the Basenji is just as capable, if not more capable, than the Sheltie of learning, why is it so devilishly hard to get a Basenji to actually do what we want them to do? The answer is that traditional training models were designed with the biddable dog (like the Sheltie) in mind. Those methods rely heavily on "showing" or "telling" the dog what to do. If you have a dog who is pre-programmed through hundreds or thousands of years of breeding to be receptive to being told what to do, those methods might get you somewhere. If you have a dog who has only ever been bred to think for himself, you will find yourself beating your head against a wall. *The problem is not the dog, but the method used to teach him.* Instead of compelling or showing the dog what you want him to do, you need to learn a system of training that will tap into your dog's ability to excel at independently motivated problem solving, just like the dogs in Fuller and Scott's study.

Please note that the fact that the Sheltie was reluctant to problem solve does not mean that the Sheltie was more or less intelligent than the other dogs. It only means that the Sheltie had a natural preference to be told what to do in that context. I think we must be careful not to ascribe labels like "intelligent" or "unintelligent" to dogs, because the assessment of a dog's intelligence is going to depend on your preconceived notions of what a dog "should" be. Stick to thinking about what you want your dog to do and the best way to get him to do it. Diagnosing a dog as "intelligent" or "unintelligent" will not further your training program in any way and will only add unnecessary baggage to the process.

OK, now let's look at your dogs learning strengths and challenges. Your Pigs Fly dog may or may not have all of these qualities, but he probably has most of them:

Strengths:
- He is lively and very interested in his surroundings.

- He is a good independent worker and problem solver.

- Once he decides he wants something, he is obsessed about getting it and capable of overcoming amazing obstacles to reach his goal.

Challenges:
- He does not care much if you approve or disapprove of what he is doing—he has no natural desire to please you.

- He has no natural inclination to pay attention to you

- He is so obsessed with doing his own thing that it is hard or impossible to get him to refocus on the thing you would like him to do.

What you will see is that your dog's strengths and obstacles are flip sides of the same coin:
- He is lively and interested in his surroundings, which means that his whole world does not hinge upon you and whether you approve of him or not.

- He is good at solving problems on his own, therefore he is doesn't need to pay attention to you much.

- He is capable of great passion and obsession toward reaching a goal, which is a fabulous thing, so long as your goals and his goals are the same.

Keep these two-sided traits in mind as you train your dog. These are the qualities that made you fall in love with him in the first place, and we are going to respect and celebrate these qualities every step of the way. An exasperating trait always has a flip side—it is the job of a good trainer to find that flip side and use it to his advantage!

2

Working Without a Net
Understanding the "Pigs Fly" Training System

I am going to tell you a dirty secret about dog training. Only about 10% of dog training is about training any particular behavior, like sit, down, or come. The other 90% of dog training is about getting your dog in a frame of mind where he is willing and able to pay attention and learn. Your average Golden Retriever or Sheltie is in, or close to being in, the frame of mind necessary to learn behaviors. Your Pigs Fly dog is not. That is why, despite the fact that there are any number of very good positive dog training books which show you how to train the basics, like sit, down, and come, most people who own Pigs Fly kinda dogs cannot get their dogs to perform with any reliability. Their dogs are just not engaged in the process.

First you have to teach your dog to want to work. You don't need to nag your dog, he can learn to offer to do things for you.

One Foot in Front of Another
Steps to Success

It is very important that you realize your primary task is to shape your dog's mindset, not train any particular behavior. Once you have your dog in the correct frame of mind, you can teach him anything in short order. Most people head to the bookstore or to training class because they want their dog to learn the canon of pet obedience—sit, down, stay, come, loose leash walking, and polite greeting rituals. As you go through this book, you will see that we don't begin with teaching those behaviors. We begin with lots of learning games that may seem irrelevant to you. You will find that sometimes we take a very long time to teach a behavior when there might be a way to teach it more quickly. There is a reason for this. The games we play and the way we teach them will fundamentally begin to change the way your dog thinks and prepare him to learn anything you want him to learn. You have to bear with me and take your dog systematically through the process. Remember, the non-biddable breeds in Scott and Fuller's study performed better than the "easy to train" breeds when presented with a problem that they had to figure out on their own. Under the Pigs Fly system, whenever possible, we are going to hand the problem over to the dog and give him room to do what he naturally does best—think it out.

Here is a summary of the steps I will take you through in this book:

1. Discover How Dogs Learn

You need to have a basic understanding of the laws of learning. Training your dog is like a card game where you hold all the "consequence" cards and your dog holds all the "behavior" cards. Learning the rules of how to get your dog to trade his "behavior" cards for your "consequence" cards is the first step.

2. Learn To Use the Clicker

The clicker is a small noise-making device that communicates to your dog that he has performed something correctly. The clicker is your power tool to communicate with your dog.

3. Get Your Dog to Offer

Your goal is to get your dog to start offering to do stuff for you without being asked. Although the exercises in this section may seem like silly games with no practical application, this is actually the most crucial section of the book. The big divide between the average Labrador and the average Fox Terrier is that the Labrador is often looking for ways to do what you want, whereas the Fox Terrier is looking for ways to get the heck away from you and do what he wants. Doing the exercises in this part can shape the Fox Terrier to think more like the Labrador.

4. Shaping

You are going to learn to get your dog to do things in small steps, using only the clicker and some rewards—the ultimate "hands free" training. This is the section where you may be thinking that there are much easier ways to teach your dog to do things, but remember, 90% of teaching a Pigs Fly dog is about shaping attitude, and only 10% is about the behaviors. Shaping is the best way to capitalize on your dog's superior problem solving ability.

5. Reinforcers

Figure out what gets your dog really excited. Get control of those things or activities. Dole them out in exchange for the things you want. Through that association, you will transfer the passion your dog feels for activities like sniffing, digging, or running away from you, to the behaviors you want, like walking on a loose leash, sitting, or coming when called.

6. Attention

Before you can do anything, your dog has to be paying attention to you. Once you go through the first steps, your dog will have pretty good attention, but we want to expand that to attention everywhere, even with monumental distractions.

7. Playing

Play is a great relationship builder. If your dog loves to play with you, he will generally be more interested in you and what you are doing. Furthermore, you want your dog to love to play with you so you can use it as a reward in exchange for things that you want. In this part of the Pigs Fly training system, you will learn lots of games and how to get even the most reluctant dog to play with you.

8. Behaviors

Here it is! This is the section on teaching your dog the actual behaviors, like sit, down, stay, and come, as well as how to change "problem" behaviors.

9. Living With Your Dog

Finally, we will discuss how to incorporate training into your life with the minimum of inconvenience to you.

Consequences, Schmonsequences
Tools We Use to Train in This System

Every training method uses the same fundamental technique—the dog does a behavior, and there is a consequence for it. If the consequence is something the dog likes, the dog will tend to do the behavior again. If the consequence is not something the dog likes, the dog will tend to not do that behavior again. The only fundamental difference between training methods is what kind of consequences the trainer chooses to use. There are four possible consequences for any action:

1. Something is added that the dog likes. For example, the dog sits and receives a cookie. This is called **positive reinforcement**.

2. Something the dog likes is taken away. For example, the dog jumps on you and you turn around and ignore him—attention is taken away. This is called **negative punishment**.

3. Something the dog does not like is added. For example, the dog gets ahead of the handler and receives a jerk on the leash. This is called **positive punishment**.

4. Something the dog does not like is taken away. For example, the dog's ear is pinched until he picks up the dumbbell—picking up the dumbbell makes the pain of the ear pinch go away. This is called **negative reinforcement**.

How, when, and if you use these four kinds of consequences will determine your ultimate success in training your dog, so it is worth your while to take a little time to think about them and understand what they mean in practical terms.

As used in behavioral science, "positive" and "negative" do not mean "good" and "bad." Positive simply means *adding* something, and negative means *taking away* something. Likewise, "reinforcement" and "punishment" have very specific meanings in this context. Reinforcement means anything that will tend to increase behavior, and punishment means anything that will tend to decrease behavior. Here are two examples that help illustrate these definitions. For most dogs, adding cookies when they sit will tend to get them to sit more often. Thus it is positive because you added cookies, and reinforcement because it increased the behavior of sitting—positive reinforcement. If, instead of giving a cookie when the dog sits, you smacked him with a newspaper, the dog will think twice about sitting again with you around. The newspaper is added, therefore it is positive, and the behavior of sitting is decreased, therefore it is punishment—positive punishment.

"Reinforcement" and "Punishment" are tricky concepts. What you have to remember is that reinforcement is anything that tends to increase behavior, while punishment is anything that tends to decrease behavior. What is a reinforcer and what is a punisher will depend on the dog's opinion. For instance, you may think that, if your dog is barking in his crate in the other room, it is punishment if you run in there and yell at him. If the dog was barking because he did not want to be isolated, your running into the room (even in an angry way) is reinforcing because the dog got what he wanted—i.e., not to be alone. Since barking worked to end his isolation, he will do it again next time. In this case, yelling at the dog was a reinforcer, since the dog's barking will increase. Conversely, you may think that, if your dog sits, giving your dog a nice scratch behind the ears is reinforcing. If, however, your dog is afraid of having his head touched (maybe he was hit in the face at a previous home, or maybe he is just shy) he will avoid doing the thing that led to the ear scratch—in this case sitting. Thus, the friendly ear scratch is punishment because it will decrease the behavior of sitting.

The key concept is that you cannot make any assumptions about what is reinforcing or punishing to your dog. You have to relax and observe how your dog is reacting to things to know what is reinforcing/punishing to him. This is unbelievably difficult for people to do. Our cultural/species biases are so profound that we find it hard to see clearly what our dogs find reinforcing/punishing. We think that yelling at our dog for barking is punishment and we think that a scratch behind the ear is reinforcing, so it takes some patience and practice to see beyond our assumptions.

I have found that you get the best performance and most enthusiasm for training out of Pigs Fly dogs by relying on positive reinforcement as much as possible and, to a much lesser extent, negative punishment. If you are setting up and managing your dog correctly, he will be offering you lots of behaviors that you can reinforce, and there will be very few times when he is not doing what you want. When your dog does something right, he is rewarded. When he does something that you do not want him to do, he is ignored, reinforcements are withheld, or he is given a time-out. This is the technique that is used to train killer whales to swim in a tank without eating the other animals, pee in a cup, and hold their mouths open for dental attention. Can you imagine giving a correction to a Killer Whale? If an undomesticated, ten thousand pound marine mammal can be trained without correction, you can train your family's Fox Terrier without correction.

How far do you think she would get if she tried to compel or correct this whale? If we can train wild Killer Whales without coercion, we can train dogs without coercion.

You Can't Go Anywhere if There is No Gas in the Tank
Creating an Operant Dog

The owner of the easy-to-train dog has a head start on you. Those dogs actually find their owner's approval to be reinforcing. Your dog, on the other hand, really does not care if you approve of him or not. Before you even get started training, your dog has to want to work. Those biddable dogs are just sitting there waiting for their owner's next command while your dog is doing any of hundreds of activities that are incompatible with working—sniffing, snoring on the couch, barking at squirrels, hiding behind your legs, staring off into space, etc. How are you going to teach your dog anything if he couldn't care less about you and what you have to offer? It does not matter if your dog is so shy that he is shaking in his boots, so hyper that he is ready to explode or so lazy that he has to be dragged from the couch, your first task is the same. Your dog must become **operant** before you can get anywhere with training. Whoa, hey, I slipped in a scientific term! All operant really means in the context of dog training is that:

1. The dog realizes that he gets a reward if he does something that you want and,

2. He tries to get those rewards by offering you different behaviors.

Pig-tionary

Operant: Behavior or responses that operate on the environment to produce rewarding and reinforcing effects. (Webster's Third New International Dictionary, Unabridged, 1993). Psychologist and researcher B.F. Skinner coined this term in connection with his research on laboratory rats. He placed them in a box where, if they pressed a lever, food would appear. At first the rats understandably just sort of rambled around in the box—they had no idea that there was anything they could do to create a wonderful consequence like getting food. However, once they discovered that pressing a lever made food appear, they would not only keep pressing that lever for food, but, if the lever did not work, they would try all kinds of other behaviors to get the food.

Here is an example to illustrate what operant means. When I was a kid, my friend had a little mixed breed dog named Stuart. Whenever you ate dinner at their house, Stuart would be right next to you, sitting there and begging for scraps. If you did not feed him, he would sit up on his hind legs. If you still did not give him anything, he would start waving his little paws in the air. That was generally when people gave in. Stuart was operant. Without anyone asking him, he would offer behaviors (first sitting, then sitting up, then waving his paws) until he hit on the one that "paid."

Is your dog operant? Take him out in a safely fenced-in area and let him loose. Just stand still, look at your dog, don't say anything, and wait. What will he do? Depending on the dog, he may just stand there, sniff around, lift his leg on something, zoom in circles—whatever he finds interesting. Chances are, he is not going to solicit your attention by offering behaviors. He is not operant. Now, if you take my dog, Ruby, and let her loose in a yard without telling her what to do, she is going to run out and start working the yard. She will sit, lie down, run over to a lawn chair, hit it with her paw, jump over a bench, and lie down. After each behavior, she will look at me to see if she is going to get a reward for it. She will keep offering any behavior she can think of until I reward her. Ruby has learned the important and abstract concept that her actions will work on her environment to produce a really great reward, and she is going to keep trying until she gets that reward. She loves this game and will bunny hop around the yard while trying to figure out what the "winning" behavior is.

It is important to note that Ruby learned to be operant, and your dog can, too. Ruby was so reluctant and slow as a young dog that she could barely be persuaded to break out of a walk, and she had no desire whatsoever to play with me. I conditioned her to become operant and to love playing this game with me more than anything else, and you can condition your dog to be operant, too.

Ruby has offered to take this jump without any prompting from me. She seems to be asking, "Is this the behavior that will pay off?"

Don't worry if, as you are reading this, you have no idea how in a million years you would ever be able to get your dog to pay attention to you and offer behaviors. That will be covered in detail later. All you need to understand from this chapter is the concept of an operant dog, and why it is central to this training system. The operant dog is like the eager Golden Retriever—waiting expectantly for your next move. You really can train your Pigs Fly dog to be that way.

You are going to train your dog to keep trying and be actively thinking. The operant dog has gotten off his duff and is on his toes, wanting to play the game. At least this gives you something to work with. I want you to walk on the edge and push the envelope. You are going to get lots of behaviors from the dog, and then hone them down to the finished behaviors you want. The process can appear to be messy and chaotic when viewed in tiny segments, but the ultimate behaviors are continually being shaped, and the result is a dog that not only does the required behaviors, but does them eagerly, with his ears up and his tail wagging. Once your dog is operant, it is easy to start shaping behaviors by reinforcing the ones you want and ignoring those you do not want.

Now that you know that the first and most important thing you need to do with your Pigs Fly dog is to get him active and operant, you can begin to understand why traditional training methods fail these dogs and why it is so important to learn to train without using corrections. Traditional training methods use a lot of positive punishment—leash corrections, verbal reprimands, physical grabbing or striking of the dog—to both shape desired behavior and control unwanted behavior. There are lots of reasons why I avoid using punishment in my training program, but the one reason that is central to this book is that, even when expertly administered (which it almost never is) punishment has a blanket dampening effect of the dog. The effect of punishment is to make your dog unwilling to try behaviors, which is the exact opposite of being operant. Sadly, many people are happy with this—they define a well-behaved dog as one that basically does not do anything. That is antithetical to the Pigs Fly training system.

I don't recommend positive punishment on any breed of dog, but some breeds/types are going to be able to take a degree of punishment and still function. For example, a particular Labrador Retriever who has a strong inclination to be interested in you and what you are doing, might put up with some punishment and still be eager to train, because his desire to be with you is a strong motivator. The Labrador, in many cases, is hanging around with interest just to see what you would do next and if, joy of joys, you might ask him to participate in your next activity. The Shar-Pei, on the other hand, really has no interest in your next inevitably pointless and stupid activity. If you punish the Shar-Pei he is going to go from neutral-not-caring to actively avoiding. If you punish your little Dachshund for chewing a shoe, he may generally freeze up in your presence and never do that, or any other behavior, in your presence again. Unfortunately, lots of people have that frozen little dog as a goal. Getting these zombie dogs to perform even desired behaviors, like sitting or coming when called, becomes next to impossible. Consider what trainer and author Jean Donaldson writes in her book, *The Culture Clash* (Berkeley: James & Kenneth, 2005):

> If you [administer punishment correctly], the punishment may buy you a temporary suppression of the behavior. Remember, you have not killed it but merely brought about an emotional state which is incompatible with the behavior you want to get rid of (the animal is too upset by the punishment to do it for the time being). He is also, incidentally, too upset to do much of anything right after a punishment. Punishment is like carpet bombing. The behavior you wanted to target gets hit but so does a huge portion of the dog's whole repertoire. *Dogs who are punished a lot behave a lot less in general.* What's particularly scary is that this is what a lot of dog owners actually want. They want a general toning down of the dog. It is a sad comment on human-dog relations when we claim to love dogs and then attempt to behaviorally lobotomize them with thousands of leash jerks in the name of "obedience." The bland, behavior less animal many people bond to so strongly can scarcely be called a dog. It is the ghost of what once might have been a dog. (Emphasis added)

This little dog is eager to try attempt a new behavior because she trusts that her owner will not correct her.

I think it is very nice that we can train our dogs without positive punishment. It does appeal to me from a humane perspective, I'll admit it. However, that is not why you need to learn to train without using corrections or positive punishment. You need to learn to train that way because it is the best way to get your dog to trust you enough to try things freely. If you can learn to train almost exclusively by rewarding your dog for doing what you do want, and eliminate luring and/or compelling the dog to do things, the dog has absolutely nothing to lose by trying again and again until he comes up with the right answer. He will continuously offer behaviors until he hits on the right one. All you have to do is cherry pick and reinforce the behaviors you want. It really is that simple (well, almost).

Dressing for the Occasion
A Note on Equipment

It is very important that you use only collars and harnesses that control your dog without delivering a punishment. I recommend a flat-buckle collar for most dogs. The only other collar I will ever use or permit in my classes is a martingale collar. Sometimes called Greyhound collars, these collars have a limited ability to tighten, but will never close so much as to choke or hurt the dog. My Bull Terriers have big necks and they can easily slip out of a buckle collar, so I use martingale-style collars. If you are afraid your dog might slip out of his collar, the martingale is the way to go. If you are put in the position of having to walk a heavy puller before the dog has been trained not to pull, there are great harnesses on the market, such as the Sense-ation™ harness. These clever harnesses hook up to a ring in the front of the harness, in the middle of the dog's chest. If the dog pulls, the energy of his pulling actually turns him around in the opposite direction from that in which he was pulling. Be aware that squirmy dogs can get out of them, so I recommend clipping the leash to both the harness and the collar.

I do not use or recommend head halters. Head halters tend to suppress behavior rather than helping you re-train it. It appears to me that many dogs find having their heads trussed up and manipulated in this way punishing. They may appear to be "good" but really they are too just miserable to do much of anything—which is what people sometimes mistakenly read as "well behaved."

Martingale collars.

This clever harness uses a dog's own strength to keep him from pulling. Because the leash is hooked to the front of the harness, a pulling dog will get turned around instead of going forward.

A determined dog can squirm his way out of a front-hook harness. Clip your leash to both the harness and the collar as insurance against an escape.

You will need a long lead ranging from ten feet to thirty feet long. Nylon leads are more durable and safe than leather or cotton web leads. This will give your dog a sense of freedom and the opportunity to make choices about behavior, while at the same time limiting his ability to run away from you.

You will also need something to hold your treats and toys while you train. You can use a fanny pack or you can buy a bait bag to clip to your waistband. Better yet, you can go to your local hardware store and get a free or inexpensive fabric nail apron. I like the nail aprons because you can store a selection of toys and different kinds of treats in the pockets.

Now that you are dressed up and ready to go, let's move on to learning how to learn!

3

Unlocking the Secrets of the Magic Plastic Box

What are Clickers and Markers?

The **clicker** is a little plastic box with a metal tongue it that makes a clicking sound when pushed and released. The clicker is used to let the dog know when he has done something right. The clicking sound is of no significance to an untrained dog. We must invest the click with a pleasurable meaning by associating it with food rewards. In order to make the click mean something to the dog, we start by clicking and then delivering a treat right after the click, again and again. After a short while, our dogs figure out that the clicking sound always means food, and that makes dogs love the sound of the clicker.

Once the relationship of click and treat is imbedded in our dog's minds, we can use the click to **mark** any behavior we like. When I say "mark," what I mean is that when the dog does something that we want him to do, we click the clicker to mark the behavior so the dog knows that he got it right and will be getting a treat for it—it is just a highly efficient way of saying "That's right!" Dogs quickly learn to crave the sound of the clicker and will work hard to find ways to make you give them a click.

From left to right: traditional box-type clicker; a small novelty clicker, good for children with small hands; and an I-click™ clicker, good for people with long nails or arthritis.

The choice of what kind of clicker to use will depend on you and your dog. Clickers come in a variety of shapes and sizes and they vary in how loud they are. Most have recessed metal tongues that you need to press firmly to make the clicking sound. There are also clickers with raised buttons on them—very helpful for people with long fingernails, arthritis, or large fingers. Some dogs are frightened or startled by the sound of the click at first. There are many different types of clickers and not all of them make as loud a noise as the original box-type. If your dog is not comfortable even with one of the quieter clickers, wrap it up in a small towel to muffle the sound to start. Since we will be pairing the sound of the clicker with food rewards, in no time at all the click will actually make your dog happy and content when he hears it. For additional information on clicker training, see the Resources section at the end of the book.

Non-sense Makes the Most Sense for Training
Why You Should Use a Clicker

Why use a clicker at all? Say you want to teach your dog to run next to you and go through the middle of a tire suspended off the ground, like those used in agility. It may seem obvious to you that going through the middle of the tire is the correct behavior, but it's not obvious to your dog. He could run around it to the left, run around it to the right, go underneath it, or jump through it. Jumping through it is only one of four possibilities, and it is the most difficult one to do. You line your dog up and move him towards the tire. He goes around it. You do nothing. He goes under it. You do nothing. He goes through it and a-hah! He hears the click (which is really shorthand for "a goodie is coming"), and he knows that jumping through the tire is what you want.

Clicking and treating at the right time can result in the behavior you desire. Just ignore other behaviors and reward what you want.

To use an example that is more practical for most people, say you want to teach your dog to lie down on a nice fluffy dog bed in a corner while you sit on the couch and watch TV. It may seem obvious to you that the dog is supposed to go lie down on that dog bed on which you have spent so much money, but he has no idea what you want. There are at least three other corners in the room, plus lots of comfy furniture, not to mention the thick oriental carpet under the coffee table and that nice little niche behind the armchair. He has lots of choices and the dog bed may or may not be the most attractive one. By clicking when your dog is actually on that bed, you can communicate to him that this is where you want him to be, and that good things happen when he is in that spot.

Could you just use a marker word like "Yes" or "Good" instead of using the clicker? Sure, but it is much less clear. The click is a completely artificial noise and has no pre-existing meaning for the dog. Thus, once you condition your dog to understand that the click equals goodie, that sound will always and only mean that. Your voice, no matter how odd a marker word you use, will never be as clear. No matter how skilled you are, no matter how hard you try to make your marker word sound exactly the same each time, there will always be nuances of meaning any time you say a word. This will slow down the learning process. This is not to say that you will never use verbal markers or that you will have to train everything using a clicker. Verbal markers (such as "Yes") are necessary, too. You won't always have a clicker on you and you never want to miss the opportunity to mark a desirable behavior. However, for formal training sessions when you are introducing your dog to new things, the clicker is indispensable.

Another advantage of the clicker over a spoken word is that the dog's central nervous system can process the click many times faster than it can process a word. A spoken word must be recognized and interpreted before the dog understands that a behavior is being marked. In contrast, a click is processed almost instantaneously.

Karen Pryor and veterinary neurophysiologist Barbara Schoening have been doing some research into the neuropsychology of clicker training in an attempt to discover exactly why clickers do work so well. Their hypothesis is that the click is processed in a different part of the brain than spoken words are. The click, they believe, goes directly to the instinctive, reflexive, part of the brain (the amygdala, which is part of the limbic system) instead of having to go to the "thinking" part of the brain (the cortex). According to Pryor in an article entitled *The Neurophysiology of Clicker Training*:

> Research in neurophysiology has identified the kinds of stimuli—bright lights, sudden sharp sounds—that reach the amygdala first, before reaching the cortex or thinking part of the brain. The click is that kind of stimulus. Other research, on conditioned fear responses in humans, shows that these also are established via the amygdala, and are characterized by a pattern of very rapid learning, often on a single trial, long-term retention, and a big surge of concomitant emotions….Barbara and I hypothesize that the clicker is a conditioned 'joy' stimulus that is acquired and recognized through those same primitive pathways, which would help explain why it is so very different from, say, a human word, in its effect.

Once a dog is properly conditioned on the clicker, he will react to the clicker reflexively. He literally cannot help but respond. I don't know anyone who has conditioned a verbal marker (such as "yes" or "good") to such a high degree. The clicker is definitely a power tool!

Piggy Pointer

You can get clickers on cords that you can wear around your neck, or a clicker that is attached to a springy cord that you can wear as a bracelet. You won't have to wear it forever, but it helps if you always have a clicker on you when you are trying to capture a new behavior. I have clickers stashed in every room of my house—windowsills are great places to keep clickers.

Getting Loaded
How to Power Up the Clicker

In this exercise we are going to "load" the clicker, so that the dog knows what it means. Do this exercise at home at first. You want the environment to be a relatively boring for the dog so that the exercise is very interesting by comparison. Start with about 20 very small pieces of really yummy treats. The treats should be relatively small and soft so that the dog can eat them quickly. We are going to be doing some rapid repetitions of this exercise and we don't want to have to wait for the dog to chew up a hard biscuit in between each rep. Hot dogs, cheese, ham, baked liver, and cut up chicken or steak are all popular training treats. Dried salmon is great for finicky dogs. Use something your dog goes crazy for—no dry kibble or other boring dog food. If you have a dog that does not relish food treats he is probably overfed. Try fasting him for a day (it's good for him if he is otherwise healthy) and see if he is more interested in the treats after that. If your dog absolutely will not work for food, try toys or verbal praise or a head scratch.

Treats should be large enough to serve as a reward, but you don't want the dog to get full during a training session. Even the largest dog does not need a treat cut larger than a nickel.

Place a bunch of treats in one hand and the clicker in the other. Click. Shove a treat in your dog's mouth really quickly, within one half second of the click. You want to time the click and the treat very closely together when you are starting out so the dog makes an association between the two things. Do that about 20 times. Your pattern should be: click/treat, wait a beat; click/treat, wait a beat; click/treat, wait a beat; and so forth. We are conditioning the dog to have an almost involuntary response to the clicker, and many repetitions are needed to do this.

Why do you need to deliver the treat so quickly after the click when just starting out? That is because scientific studies have proved that a reinforcement has to be delivered within a half second of a new behavior in order to have the maximum effectiveness.

When you are powering up the clicker, be certain that the click comes before the treat. Remember, we want the click to be sound that tells the dog that he is going to be getting a treat. If your dog has heard the click immediately *before* the treat many, many, times, what do you think the click predicts for your dog? A treat, of course! If your dog has heard the click *after* the treat many, many, times, then what do you think the click predicts for your dog? Nothing! The click has to come before the treat to have any meaning for the dog.

Click and treat twenty times, twice a day for three days. By the end of the third day, I can guarantee you that your dog will get whiplash when he hears the click. That's when you know the clicker is powered up.

Once the clicker is conditioned in this way, you will no longer need to get the treat to the dog so quickly. Now the clicker can serve as a **bridge** to mark the correct behavior with surgical precision, and then you can give the dog a treat in a relatively relaxed fashion. You need this kind of bridge to be an effective trainer.

What the clicker has allowed you to do is expand that ½ second of time between behavior and the reward into a few seconds by using the clicker as a bridge. You still want to try to click as soon as you can after the behavior occurs, but now the treat delivery can lag a few seconds. So long as the clicker is strongly powered up, the better the chance the dog will understand what he did to earn that treat. Without a bridge like a clicker, it is very difficult to make your dog understand what he is being rewarded for, and chances are you might end up reinforcing the wrong behavior. Take the example of sitting. You may think, if you feed within five seconds of your dog sitting, you have reinforced the sit. However, in the dog's mind, he may have done at least four things in those intervening seconds between the sit and the treat. Here is what the list looks like in the dog's mind:

1. Sit

2. Lick chops

3. Wag tail

4. Turn head away to the left

If you have not marked the "sit" with either a clicker or a verbal bridge (like "Yes!"), and you feed the dog after three seconds when he has just done number four, the head turn, what have you reinforced? Turning head away to the left! Can you see how, without a powerful marker that serves as a bridge, you may actually be training something other than you thought you were? Does this explain for you why sometimes your dog appears to perversely do something completely different than you have "trained" him to do?

The technical term for what you are doing in this section is "creating a **conditioned reinforcer** by using **classical conditioning**." What a mouthful. All it really means is that you have taken something that has absolutely no meaning to the dog (the click) and paired it with something really good (the treat) again, and again, and again, and again, until the dog actually begins to equate the meaningless thing (the click) with the really great thing (the food). The result is that when the dog hears the conditioned reinforcer (the click) his body will actually respond as if food is present—the parasympathetic nervous system kicks in and sends out signals for the dog to relax and feel happy in expectation of the food. Remember Pavlov and the dog who drooled when he heard the bell? That's classical conditioning. So, once you have finished loading the clicker, you have the ability to reward you dog not just with food, but with a whole feeling of happiness and contentment. How cool is that?

How did you do on this exercise? Was it easy? Were you all thumbs? Don't feel bad if you were. You will get much better at handling the clicker with just a little practice. I have a friend who, when she first started with the clicker, used to try to click the food and feed the clicker to her dog! It takes some time to get used to the clicker, but don't worry, it will quickly become so easy to use that you won't even have to think about it. If you were using a regular box-type clicker, you might often pick it up facing the wrong way, and when you try to click it nothing will happen because you will be pressing on the non-flexible end of the metal tongue. This is especially frustrating when you quickly grab the clicker from your pocket and then miss clicking a great behavior because the clicker is facing the wrong way in your hand. You can, however, tell if the clicker is facing the right way in your hand without looking at it by very slightly depressing the tongue without actually clicking it—if it does not have any give you know you need to face it the other way. In no time at all it becomes second nature to feel for that spring of the metal tongue so you know you are holding it correctly.

You Rang?
Awesome Name Recognition

The first thing I teach any dog after powering up the clicker is name recognition. I want my dog to get really excited when he hears his name. Name recognition is not the same as a recall. A recall means "come to me" but a dog's name means "be alert, because we are going to do something now." The majority of my dogs' lives are spent just being a dog—hanging out, sleeping, chewing a bone. When I say a name, that dog knows that he is "on duty" and I have his full attention. Also, when you think about it, all the words that we use as a cue for behaviors, like "sit," "stay," and "down," are words that we use every day in conversation. By teaching our dogs their name, we create a "qualifier" word. That is to say, if you are talking to someone and you say, "I fell down," your dog understands that no action is required on his part. If you say, "Fluffy, down," Fluffy understands that it is time for him to actually lie down.

If you have multiple dogs, names mean "What comes next (sit, come, roll over, etc.,) applies to you, Fluffy, and you, Spike and Spot, can chill out until I address you directly." For instance, if you have three dogs in your back yard and want to take just one of them out through a gate, you have two options. Option one is to put a leash on the dog you want to take out and open the gate a crack. If you are lucky, all three dogs will press their noses to the crack, and you can start shoving with your feet at the two that you want to remain. If you have small dogs you might actually be able to lift them up with your foot and toss them a good distance away. Next, open the gate and hope that the dog you want to go through does so quickly, before the other two can recover and storm the gate. If you are skinny and fast, you might be able to slip through the gate after him and turn around in time to start shoving the other two with your feet as you close the gate on your ankle. Cursing is optional. If you are not skinny and fast, you can use your body as sort of a plug to block the opening as you move through in a crouched position, while continuing to kick backwards with your feet as you move through. Option two is to teach your dogs to wait inside the yard until you call them out by name—you won't get a cardio-vascular work out as you would with option one, but it is much easier. My dogs will line up in a sit-stay on one side of a gate and I can say, "Nicky, stay. Ruby, stay. Augie, come." Without name recognition, this would be impossible.

It is easiest to start powering up your dog's name right after 20 reps of just clicking and treating. He is going to be staring at you at that point, anyway, so you can take advantage of that and pair his name with the click. While the dog is looking at you, say his name, click and treat. Do that 10-20 times in a row. After three days of this, you will be very gratified to see how fast your dog's head swivels around when he hears his name. Congratulations—your dog knows his name.

Now that you have taken the first step and trained your dog to realize that his name is of significance, you have to be careful not to un-do the work you have put in by coupling your dog's name with anything that is unpleasant. If you want to preserve the great name recognition that you have built with your clicker, your dog's name has to be a truly sacred sound. By "sacred," I mean that his name has to be the sound that he treasures hearing over any other sound in the world. In order to do this, you have to be sure that the only time he ever hears his name is when a good consequence is to follow. In your daily interactions with your dog, his name must always be connected to something good. Once it looks to you like your dog understands that his name is the greatest word ever spoken, you won't have to give him treat every time he hears his name, but you should at the very least have a warm smile ready.

Both of these dogs know their names. I can ask Augie to stay while I ask Nicky to come through the gate. Both dogs will get nice treats for these behaviors.

Never call your dog's name and then scold him or do something he does not like. This is so especially important with a Pigs Fly kind of dog. When Timmy called Lassie's name, Lassie heard it and, without any further prompting, responded from three counties away, at significant peril to her life. When you call your dog's name, you will see him running his risk/benefit equation and deciding whether it is in his interest to look at you or not. He is not going to cut you any slack in that equation. On one side of the balance sheet is a great big world, with all the interesting smells, sights, and sensations that God put there. On the other side all you have is the meaning you have invested in your dog's name through history of reinforcement or punishment. What is in the history of your dog's name? Cookies? Wow, that's better than sniffing dirt! Rides in the car? Chasing squirrels is not nearly as fun as a car ride! Leash walks? Digging a hole does not compare with a leash walk! Medicine being put in ears? Whoops, lying in this patch of sun at the far side of the yard sounds pretty good right now.

4

Shape, Rattle, and Roll

Fundamentals of Shaping Behaviors

In this chapter you are going to learn a fun and effective way to teach your dog new skills using a process called "shaping." **Shaping** involves slicing the behavior you want your dog to do into tiny pieces, successively clicking and treating each "slice," until you have built up the finished behavior you want to train.

Here is how shaping works. Imagine you are looking at a frame-by-frame motion picture of your dog picking up a tennis ball. What would the first frame be? Probably turning his eyes towards the ball. Then maybe a direct stare at the ball. Then lowering his head towards the ball. Then about six more frames where his head gets progressively lower and lower. Then touching his nose to the ball, then opening his mouth, then putting his mouth around the ball, then closing his mouth around the ball, then lifting his head for about six more frames. Each of these "frames" is called an **approximation**—a little step towards the finished behavior of picking up a ball. If you want to teach your dog to pick up a ball by shaping it, you progressively click and treat all of the "approximations" that I have described above in this way:

1. The first step is the dog turning his eyes towards the ball. After you have clicked and treated that glance toward the ball a couple of times, your dog will start offering it. By "offering it," I mean he will deliberately glance towards the ball in an attempt to make the clicker go off.

2. Once your dog is firmly and deliberately offering the glance towards the ball, you can hold out and not click it. Your dog will keep trying the glance, and then, when he sees that it is not paying off, he will offer "improvements" on that behavior, like a bit of a head turn in that direction. Voila! You have frame number two, the head turn, which you can start click and treating.

3. Again, once your dog is firmly and deliberately offering the head turn, hold out for any tiny lowering of his head. Click and treat that a few times, and then, when you are sure he is offering a bit of a head bob, hold out for a

bigger head bob. Again, when reinforcements are not forthcoming, your dog will offer different "improvements" on the head bob, which will eventually include lowering his head toward the ball more than he had before. You continue this way, reinforcing and then holding out for more through the rest of the "frames" of the "movie" of your dog picking up the ball.

As you can see, even a simple behavior like picking up a ball is actually a series of many small behaviors. Your fun challenge as a trainer is to learn to recognize and reinforce each little step until you build the finished behavior.

Piggy Pointer

It might really only take a couple of approximations to get your dog to do a behavior, depending on the dog and the behavior you are trying to teach. As you become more experienced, however, you will find that the more approximations you reinforce, the better and faster your dog will learn, remember, and perform the behavior.

It is very important that you do not prompt, lure, or, compel/guide your dog to do anything. Your dog is going to learn to offer to do things for you without you asking. Offering to do things is not something that comes naturally to most Pigs Fly dogs, but you can teach it. The first exercise we will do is to get your dog hip to the rules of the game—he does all the work and you let him know when he has it right.

Shaping without prompting/luring/compelling your dog to do anything (also called "**free shaping**") is central to the Pigs Fly system. Your dog needs a work ethic, and this is going to teach him to have one. You just can't train a dog that does not want to try. Remember, your dog is the one who excelled at independent problem solving. The "Pigs Fly" breeds learned more quickly than the "easy to train" Sheltie when they were not told what to do, but had to figure it out by themselves. If you push on your dog's butt to get him to sit, lure him around with a piece of food, or jerk on his collar to get him to stop pulling, you are not using his natural way of thinking to your advantage. Sure, you might get him to do what you want him to do, but it will be a long, cold, slog up a very steep hill. By free shaping him to do things, you can take your "who cares?" dog and make him as crazy to do things for you as a Border Collie. Don't believe me? Let's give it a try!

Pig-tionary

Free Shaping: Training behaviors by rewarding small approximations of those behaviors without the use of luring or prompting. B.F. Skinner coined the term "shaping" in connection with his work on laboratory rats. Dog trainer Deb Jones, PhD, expanded the term to "free shaping" to emphasize the absence of prompting, luring, or compulsion.

The focus of this first lesson is on you and your ability to pick out and take a picture of a behavior with a clicker. The Pigs Fly training system deliberately begins with playing games rather than training "useful" behaviors so that you can concentrate on your mechanical training skills and your dog can concentrate on becoming operant. Actual training behaviors you will use, like sit, come, and down, will come later. First you must take that most crucial step on which 90% of dog training success depends: creating a dog who wants to work. If you begin by training "useful" behaviors, you are likely to get caught up in "getting it right" and the sessions will not be as free or mentally productive for you and your dog. Our goal by the end of this lesson is that:

1. You will be fluent enough with the clicker that you will be able to mark the desired behavior with some accuracy, and;

2. You dog will have opened up and started to offer behaviors continuously.

Don't be discouraged if you find it hard at first to coordinate your clicking with the exact behavior you want to mark. Everyone starts out a little clumsy—remember my friend who kept trying to click the food and feed the clicker to her dog! You will get the hang of it, I promise. You will get better and better at it until the click becomes an automatic response that you do not have to think about.

If you want to do some "extra credit" work on your clicker skills, you could practice while watching TV—pick one behavior and click that. You could click for nods, or smiles, or tosses of the hair, handshakes, whatever. You don't need to practice in this way, but some people enjoy it and it is helpful. Either way, you will be pleasantly surprised at how quickly your timing improves.

If you did lesson one, you have a dog that stares at you every time you pick up a clicker. Now you are going to go for something more.

Thinking About the Box
Your Dog's First Learning Game

Do you remember playing a game when you were a kid where a friend hid something and you had to find it only by moving around the room while your friend gave you hints by saying "Warm – warmer – colder – warmer – red hot!" That is exactly the game you are going to play with your dog. For this exercise, we are going to use an empty cardboard box. The exact size and shape of the box is not particularly important, but it should be low enough for the dog to step into easily, and large enough to fit at least two of his feet in, if he wishes. A shirt box will do nicely for most dogs. Here are the rules:

1. The object of the game is to have your dog interact with the box in any way he pleases. Touch it with his nose, paw at it, step in it, pick it up in his mouth, sit in it—it makes absolutely no difference what the behavior is. As long as he interacts with the box, he gets clicked. You may say "yes!" or "good!" after you click as a reinforcement in addition to the treat, but you may not say anything to help him along. Just like in the "warm, warmer" game, you are restricted to the clicker to tell the dog if he is getting close.

2. Do nothing if your dog is getting "colder." No helping allowed! This game is about your dog figuring it out on his own.

3. After your dog has offered any interaction with the box and you have clicked it, you may throw the treat in the box to reinforce that the box is a "hot" area. Only throw the treat in after clicking, though—don't throw the treat in the box to lure him towards it!

As soon as you put the box down, be ready to click—there is hardly a dog in the world that will not investigate something you put on the ground in front of him. Then click any interaction at all with the box. As you can see, this is a very enjoyable game that makes dogs eager to offer to do things for you.

To begin the game, hold the box in one hand and the clicker in the other. Make sure the clicker is facing the right way in your hand and you are ready to click. Put the box down on the floor. Most likely, your dog will investigate the box by touching it with his nose the second you put it down. Click immediately! If your dog does not touch the box with his nose, but just looks towards it, click that and drop the treat into the box. By clicking him for just looking at the box, you are saying "warm!" Wait for him to interact with the box again. Click any interaction, even if it is not the same one as before. Click and treat him even if he accidentally touches the box. Here are some tips to help you:

1. If your dog just stands there like a lump, staring at you, wait it out for a long time. If you really can't stand it longer, walk around the box so your dog will accidentally touch it and click that. Looking pointedly back and forth between your dog and the box also helps.

2. Try putting your hands behind your back when you want your dog to free shape. This helps in two ways. First, if the dog can see the food and clicker in your hand, he often will become fixated with it. Taking those things out of the picture helps him start thinking and stop staring. Second, putting your hands behind your back will become a cue for your dog to start offering behaviors, rather than waiting for you to tell him what to do.

3. If your dog acts shy or afraid of the box, you have two options. If the shyness is not severe, just click for looking at the box or any movement at all towards the box. If your dog is really spooked by the box, just use something else less threatening. Try a rope toy, a book, a food dish, or anything at all that your dog is not frightened of. This exercise is not about getting any particular behavior, so it does not matter what you use.

4. If your dog runs wildly around and seems not to notice the box at all, just click him for being in the same room as the box, then in the same half of the room as the box, then in the same 5 foot square as the box, and so forth, until he is interacting with the box. If your clicker has been powered up sufficiently, your dog will catch on to the game very quickly.

Continue to click and treat for any interaction with the box for the entire session—a glance, a sniff, a lick, a paw in or on the box, a mouth on the box, anything at all!

Some dogs are just gifted at this game and will be merrily interacting with the box in only three or four clicks. Some dogs will take five minutes before they even try to move out of one spot. Don't get discouraged. Accept what your dog gives you and work with it. Don't worry if your dog seems to be a slow learner. Every dog catches on, eventually.

A little dog like this might find it intimidating to interact with a box, so you could try using a rope toy, instead. Here, I am clicking her for looking at the rope toy and then for touching it with her nose.

As a rule, your free shaping sessions should be quite short. Five to ten minutes is a nice amount of time to spend in a training session of this sort. The most ideal training schedule would be three five minute sessions spread out over the course of a day, but one session per day is just fine, too.

When you can bet $100 that your dog will immediately start offering behaviors when you put the box down, you can add a **cue**, such as, "What can you do", or, "Gimme something" to signal the start of your free-shaping session. It might take one session or ten sessions to get to this point. Don't rush and don't be frustrated. Enjoy the process and let your dog learn at his own pace.

Pig-tionary
Cue: A stimulus which sets the occasion for a particular response. A cue, sometimes called a command, is a verbal signal that you give your dog to do a particular behavior, like "sit," "down," or "come."

When your dog begins hustling around and offering behaviors as soon as you put the box down and say "What can you do?" move on to the next exercise. Do not be in a hurry; we want your dog really happy about and crazy over this box before you move on.

Pig Tale
My dog Ursa was introduced to the clicker as an adult and it took her a very long time to start offering behaviors. We could not play the "box" games, because she would just stand there, completely inert, and stare at me. When she tired of this, she would walk away. I would end the session at that point, thinking she was uninterested and did not get it. Sometime around the third session, I clicked her just as she turned her head to walk away, but before she actually took a step. She got her treat, and then stood there and stared at me for another few minutes. When she turned away again, I clicked. That first session was mighty painful and long, but that was a turning point for her. After that, Ursa started offering

a head turn during our shaping sessions. We built on that in tiny increments, and it was not long before she was playing the box game with enthusiasm. The moral of the story is, even if the only thing your dog will do is walk away from you—click it!

The Journey Begins With One Footstep
How to Shape a Behavior

Did you and your dog have fun with the "box" training game? Great! Now you are ready to take the next step and actually train something. Before, you were clicking any interaction at all with the box. Now I want you to pick out a behavior for your dog to do with the box. Some suggestions are—put a front foot in the box, touch the box with his nose,pick up the box with his teeth—anything at all as long as you determine exactly what you want him to do so you know in advance what to shape.

Since you have been playing the free shaping game with the box already, you have a pretty good idea of what behaviors your dog is likely to offer, and I recommend you start with one of those behaviors. Don't, for instance, try to shape your tightly-wrapped terrier to lie down in the box at first. Most terriers prefer to be on their feet, especially during the excitement of a training session. Similarly, don't think you are going open up with shaping your shy little Italian Greyhound to pick up the box in his mouth. On the other hand, if you happen to have a dog of the retriever family, picking the box up in his mouth would be a comfortable behavior to start with. Dogs in general seem to believe that their body ends at their shoulders, so any behavior that involves a hind leg will be a hard trick to start with. Think about your dog's nature and what you have observed in your free shaping sessions, and then try to make your first attempt at shaping a behavior a positive and successful one for you and your dog.

Have a seat in a nice armchair with your clicker in your hand and a bowl of treats next to you. Pour yourself a glass of wine for your other hand. Put your feet up, say the magic words, "What can you do?" and get ready to click. You are going to build the behavior you have selected by approximations. As we discussed earlier, rather than waiting to see the entire behavior and then clicking, you are going to break down the behavior into the tiniest steps possible and reward each of those. Slice up the behavior as if you were viewing a frame-by-frame motion picture of the behavior. For instance, let's say that you chose to shape your dog to put his front feet in the box and your set up looks like this:

You	The dog	The box

What is the tiniest approximation of the behavior of the dog putting his front feet in the box? The dog is probably standing there staring at you. The behavior of "put your front feet in the box" is really "turn away from me, take two steps away from me in the direction of the box, lift your foot near the box, lower your foot into the box." So, the very first thing that the dog needs to do is to turn his head away from you—not necessarily a big turn, just an ear flick and eye roll in that direction is enough. Click and treat the eye roll and ear flick. Do that a few times until your dog is quite obviously offering it several times in a row. Now, hold out and do not click when he offers the eye roll and ear flick. Wait for a tiny bit more. Now you want some actual turning of the head. You are not looking for a big swivel of the head, but some slight movement.

Piggy Pointer
When you throw the treat in the box after the click, you are using an important training tool—click for the behavior and treat for position. For instance, if you want your dog to sit, you should click as his butt is hitting the ground, and then feed him at nose level so he remains seated. If you always feed him in such a way that he pops up to get the treat, he will begin to anticipate the treat and pop up right after his rear hits the ground. You will have trained a bouncing dog instead of a sit. By feeding in a sit position, we are reaffirming to the dog that the "sit" is the behavior that pays.

This game works because dogs learn very quickly what gets them treats. If a head turn gets them treats, they remember that and offer it. If the head turn has been reinforced enough times they will keep offering that head turn, even if you stop reinforcing it. Dogs are hopeful creatures, and, when they figure out that the head turn does not get them treats anymore, they will start offering "improvements" on the head turn, like a head turn with foot movements. Your job is to catch those improvements and click them. The term we use for what you are doing is **raising the criteria**.

Pig-tionary
Raising Criteria: When we ask for "something more" in a behavior, we say we are "raising the criteria." So, as we approximate the head turn, the eyeball roll might be the first approximation that we reward, and then we raise the criteria to a slight head turn.

Knowing when to stop reinforcing one approximation of a behavior and hold out for more is more of an art than a science. As a general rule of thumb, if your dog looks like he is losing interest or giving up when you start holding out for an "improvement," you have probably tried to raise the bar too quickly. Go back and reinforce the behavior he was last offering a few more times. Once that behavior is strengthened by a few more reinforcements, you can try again to hold out for the next approximation.

Here I am shaping Ruby to put her front feet in the box. Each photo represents an approximation—a place where you should click. Notice that I hold my hands behind my back. If you hold a clicker and/or treats in front of you when you free shape, a novice dog may find it hard to think about anything except the stuff in your hands.

Even if your dog has not given up, but is repeatedly offering a behavior you are not looking for, you need to find a way to reinforce him, or he will lose interest and give up. Again, knowing how long to hold out will depend on your dog's personality and training, but here is a rule of thumb to get you started. If your dog has offered three behaviors and they have not been what you want, drop back on your criteria and take a little less so that, ideally, the dog gets a reward on the fourth try. For example, if you are holding out for a head turn and you only get the same old eyeball roll three times in a row, just click the eyeball roll a few more times. If you continue to hold out for more, you run the risk of the dog just giving up. Once the original (the eyeball roll in this case) behavior has been strengthened by a few more repetitions, your dog may feel confident enough to keep trying "improved" behaviors. The "rule of three" is only a very conservative generalization to get you started—you will be amazed at how quickly you will begin to read your dog and know when to raise the training criteria and how long you should hold out.

As you work with your dog, you will get to know how persistent he is and how quickly you can raise the bar and hold out for more. Many terriers have incredible persistence and will feverishly keep offering behaviors for a very long time. If you think about the single-minded determination needed for a dog to hunt down and dig up small prey animals, it makes sense that terriers will keep trying virtually until they drop. On the other hand, a cuddly Cavalier King Charles Spaniel might be absolutely horrified when you try to raise the training criteria. They are clever dogs that will do anything you ask, but they might not be eager to mentally strike out on their own. You should be more conservative about raising the criteria with a Cavalier than with a terrier.

When your dog does finally do the ultimate behavior that you are looking for, you should rejoice, yell, "Whooohooo" (or whisper it, if your dog is shy) and dole out about 20 small treats. This is known as a **jackpot** and we use it to mark a particularly great behavior. You should also use a jackpot if your dog has been thinking hard for a long time about a problem, and then solves it, even if it is not the "ultimate" behavior you are building.

Piggy Pointer

When you are jackpotting, it is much more effective to dole out 20 small treats in rapid succession than to give one large chunk of bait. Dogs will gobble just about anything that will fit into their mouth in one bite. Oddly enough, dogs have no sense of proportion, but they can count—50 tiny pieces of food is much more valuable to a dog than one softball-sized treat that they can consume in one bite.

Did you succeed in getting your dog to do the behavior you selected? If you did, congratulations! You now know how to train your dog to do anything. All you have to do now is put the behavior on cue so your dog will perform it when you ask (you will learn how to do that later in the book) and you are all set. Teaching your dog to sit, lie down, stay, and walk on a loose leash are all taught exactly the same way using the same free shaping game.

You Can't Start If You Haven't Stopped
The Release

You need a very clear way of telling your dog that the training session or behavior you are asking for is over, and he can go do as he likes. If you don't have a clear cue that your dog is free to do as he likes, he will always be guessing when he can stop doing whatever you are asking for. It is confusing and distressing for a dog not to know if he is on duty or not. He will guess at which hand movements or changes in your voice or stance he can seize upon as a cue. He will often guess wrong, and you will get annoyed at him for "blowing you off" in the middle of a training session.

If, on the other hand, you consistently require your dog to continue doing whatever it is you are asking for until you give a specific release cue, such as "OK," "Free," or "Go Be a Dog," your dog will relax and just keep working until told to stop.

The Long Road is the Quickest Way There
Why Shaping is the Better Way to Train Everyday Behaviors

Let's look at a "practical" behavior and see how to teach it. We will use "sit" as an example. Since dogs do sit frequently on their own, you could just wait for them to sit and then click that. If you put the time into playing the free shaping games in the first part of this book, you will see the light bulb above your dog's head light up, and he will start offering to sit in hope of getting you to click him. Once you would bet $100 that your dog is going to offer a sit, you can start saying "sit" when his butt is hitting the ground. Gradually, you can start saying "sit" earlier and earlier. After a few repetitions, "sit" will become a cue for the behavior.

Many of you may be shaking your heads and thinking, "That is an awful lot of trouble to go to just to teach my dog to sit. I am going to have to play all of those games, learn a bit about training, buy a clicker and learn how to use it, keep an eye on my dog and wait around for him to sit—that's a lot of time and effort. I could push down on his butt and make him learn to sit in five minutes." My answer is, yes, of course you could, but think about the dogs in Scott and Fuller's study. The non-biddable dogs beat the biddable dogs at problem solving and thinking. By compelling a sit, you are taking any thought out of the equation and relying on avoidance. The problem with this is two-fold:

1. Many non-biddable dogs are notoriously impervious to physical discomfort. Terriers in particular have extra tough skin around their head and necks in order to withstand the bites they receive when they dive underground in pursuit of vermin. You can push and pull all you like, but they are programmed not to react much to physical manipulation. A push on the butt will make little impression on them and they are unlikely to find it punishing enough to sit promptly to avoid another push on the butt.

2. If the push on the behind does succeed in getting your dog to sit, it is not going to help you train the next behavior, unless that next behavior is based on a very similar type of avoidance of physical pressure. If, on the other hand, you teach by shaping behaviors, it gets easier and easier to teach new behaviors because the dog gets more and more excited about learning and offers more behaviors and variations/improvements on those behaviors more rapidly. Again, remember that the independently thinking dogs kicked butt when they were allowed to problem solve on their own. Why not choose a training method that will play to your dog's strengths?

Some of you may still not be convinced that free shaping a behavior is worth the effort. I can just see some of you, cookie in hand, thinking, "OK, OK, so I won't push down on my dog's butt to get him to sit, but I ain't spending an hour free shaping it. Shoot, I'll just put this cookie over his head, lure his nose up, and his butt will go right down into a sit—bingo! Sit achieved in 3 seconds! Who needs to waste all of that time and effort approximating a behavior through free shaping?" Well, you would definitely get the behavior you desire that way, but you will have missed out on great benefits that will make your life easier down the line.

If you are only luring your dog, the likelihood of your dog performing any particular action is a simple calculation of how much he likes the thing you are offering, versus how difficult or unpleasant the behavior you're asking for is. Furthermore, when you are luring your dog around with a cookie, all your dog sees is that cookie. He probably has no idea whatsoever what the rest of his body is doing. So long as his mouth is oriented towards the cookie, he thinks he is in good shape. If your dog does not like cookies or toys that much, you are out of luck. It is inevitable that, many times, the reward you present will not be interesting enough for your dog to perform the desired behavior. This is especially true when you take your dog out in public. What is a piece of hot dog compared to the excitement, smell, and novelty of the entire world?

So, how do you find a reinforcer that is more exciting than anything else in the world that your dog could possibly encounter? There is no food or toy that will ever be that valuable, but the hunt for the behavior that will make the click go off can be more engaging for a dog than anything else. If you take the trouble to create excitement for the learning process through free shaping games, even a mundane reward becomes very valuable to your dog, and rewards that he really likes become very intense reinforcers.

Here is a human example that may help you understand how an exciting process can be more important than an actual goal. When you were a kid did you ever do Easter egg or treasure hunts? Do you remember how exciting they were, how pandemonium would break out when the kids were released on the hunt? Let's face it, there was never any prize on that hunt that was that great, or that the kids had not had before. None of the prizes on the hunts were things that kids were that excited about in an everyday setting, but in the context of a hunt, those children went wild to find the fairly ordinary stuff that the adults had hidden. That is the extra power that you get from free shaping—you leverage your reinforcers so that (eventually) there is nothing in the world that can trump the possibility of a training session with you.

As you start free shaping behaviors with your dog, you will see them become very excited and intensely focused on the problem at hand. The dog does not know what the answer to the problem is, but as he throws out each behavior, there is an anticipation and hope that this might be the behavior that pays. The animation that a free shaped dog displays when problem solving is very intense and can only be compared to a dog excitedly following a scent trail or foraging for food. Your dog actually is hunting for the answer that will lead to the click. Free shaping behaviors can turn even the most dud-like, scatterbrained, or just plain oblivious dog into a training maniac.

Now, let's go back to the example of luring a dog to sit. Yes, you can get the behavior much more quickly if you lure the dog into position, and your dog will even develop some excitement at the prospect of training because there is food involved, but it is no where near the intensity that free shaping behaviors will bring. Pigs Fly dogs need to be conditioned to get excited about training, and free shaping is a great way to do it.

Don't be discouraged if free shaping behaviors seem difficult at first. After you free shape the first couple of behaviors, all the others will be incredibly easy. You will be astounded at how quickly you learn to tune into the minutest movements of your dog and how well you learn to parse down behaviors into the tiniest approximations. Ultimately, I want you to free shape as many behaviors as possible, but if you are having trouble getting a behavior and want to throw in a little lure, no one is going to die. You need to make the training process fun for you as well as your dog, and you need to have success in order to have fun. As you go along in your training and get comfortable with the clicker and shaping behaviors, you will find yourself free shaping more and more.

Plenty of Pigs Fly dogs have shyness issues which complicate their already less than abundant work ethic. Free shaping can fix shyness, too. For some reason, dogs that are timid or shy seem to be made much worse by any attempt to lure, reassure, or cheerlead them on. Try some free shaping with your shy dog and you will be downright amazed at how quickly he comes out of his shell.

Economics 101
Why and When it Pays to Lure a Behavior

Sometimes luring your dog to do a behavior makes sense, especially if it is a difficult behavior like "down." Here, I am luring a dog under my knee to help get her into the "down" position.

Luring can be a valuable training tool and I do use it on occasion in my training program. It would be really hard to train a dog without any luring at all. Some behaviors are so complicated that it would take thousands of tries to shape them, and then you still might not succeed. Furthermore, sometimes the ultimate cue for the behavior is contained within the lure, so you will not have the trouble of fading the lure.

Pig-tionary
Luring: In dog training, luring means use of food or prop to manipulate a dog into desired position or behavior. Examples would be: holding a hot dog just in front of the dog's nose so he is drawn into heel position, holding a cookie over his head so he sits down, or throwing a treat into the dog's crate so he will run in after it. I do use luring to train my dogs, but there are limited instances where I will introduce it. Especially in the beginning stages, it is more important that your dog learn how to think and offer behaviors than how to do any particular behavior, and luring is not the best way to those goals. We will discuss the proper place for lures later in the book.

These are places where it is good training economy to think about using a lure. Dog trainers will debate hotly over whether free shaping or luring is the better method of training any particular behavior. To me, the real issue is what luring vs. free shaping is doing to my dog's mental underpinnings. I train dogs that have no particular interest in working with me to start with. I find that this free shaping exercise gives the best possible chance of them becoming operant. Dogs who are eager to train and offer behaviors is like money in the bank for me to buy new behaviors down the line.

Luring is appropriate, however, when the following conditions are met:

1. The dog has played a lot of free shaping games and is very operant and fluent at offering behaviors.

2. It is just darn hard to train that particular behavior without luring.

You will know when the first condition is met and your dog is operant—he will be attending you like a bellhop at a posh resort, trying to get your attention by offering behaviors.

As for the second condition, an example of a behavior that is just darn hard to train without luring would be a "down." You can free shape a down by micro-shaping very tiny approximations, but it takes an excellent eye and finely tuned clicker skills. Most people will be better off using food or a toy to lure their dog into a down.

The thing I want you to take away from this section is that you have to make a distinction between training behaviors and training attitude and work ethic. Luring is sometimes the best training economy for getting a particular behavior, but you also have to train attitude and work ethic, and free shaping is the way to do that. There is no harm in luring a behavior if you just can't seem to get it any other way, so long as you have put in the foundation work of free shaping lots of behaviors, first. Remember, dog training, especially for a Pigs Fly kinda dog, is about getting into the dog's mind, not just controlling his body!

The Strongest House is Built With Small Bricks
Why it Pays to Break Down a Behavior into Many Approximations

I have found that, the smaller the approximations you use to shape a behavior, the more durable they will be. What do I mean by durable? Under stress or in a new context, dogs will often fail to perform behaviors that we have taught them. If you have taught the behavior in one big piece then, under enough stress or distraction, the whole behavior disappears. If you have taught the behavior by reinforcing small approximations of the behavior, the behavior will usually only break down to the last or near to the last approximation that you reinforced.

Here is an example of how small approximations can create a more durable behavior. You could teach your dog to lie down with his head resting on his feet by luring him down with a cookie and not reinforcing any approximations. You could click only when his nose touched his feet, and he would eventually learn the behavior that way. However, if you take your dog to the pet supply store and it is very exciting for him, chances are he won't lie down at all; the entire behavior was learned as one piece, and it will fall as one piece. Let's say instead of luring, you taught him to lie down and rest his head on his feet by shaping each tiny approximation of the behavior, from dipping his head slightly as he is standing all the way through resting his chin on his feet. When you take your dog to the exciting pet supply store, the "lie down and rest your head on your feet" behavior might only break down to the last couple of approximations you trained; maybe he will lie down with his head lowered, but not on his feet, or maybe his head will be up, but he will still lie down.

"Be a splitter, not a lumper" is the wise advice of the great animal trainer and behaviorist, Bob Bailey. Even if you think you might be able to "get" the behavior using fewer approximations, every approximation you reinforce will make your dog understand, remember, and perform the behavior better. You may find it hard, at first, to see and reinforce small approximations. However, as you get more experienced and your dog gets more hip to the game, you will see that you can run through a series of approximations in a matter of seconds.

5

If a Tree Falls in the Forest and Your Dog is Not Listening...

Teaching Attention as a Behavior

Automatic **attention** is the mother of all behaviors and one of the first things you should teach your dog. There is no point in teaching your dog how to do things if he is going to ignore you when you ask him to do them. If your dog is off in a mentally distant land and you repeatedly call his name, you are just like static in the background to him. The only thing you will have accomplished is to devalue his name. Even if you got yourself one of the excellent dog training books out there and followed the instructions in it exactly, you would probably find that your Pigs Fly dog still doesn't perform when you want him to. That is often because he is not paying attention to you.

Lack of attention is often, sadly, the issue that causes owners to give up on their "impossible" dogs. Take heart! Training a dog to have attention is absolutely no different than training a dog to sit or come when called. You are not going to get a "gimme" when it comes to attention. You are going to have to train it like any other behavior and that means more work for you. The good news is that it can be trained and, once you have your dog's attention, anything is possible.

You are not going to teach an "attention" cue or command. Attention is going to become your dog's default behavior, and you will not have to ask for it with nagging commands. Teaching a dog a verbal cue to pay attention implies that it is OK for him not to pay attention unless he gets the verbal cue. Instead, if your dog is with you, he should be conditioned to watch you like a hawk all the time because he never knows

Attention is the foundation for any training program.

when you might do something interesting or fun. If you call your dog to you, or take him out on a leash, you should become the center of his universe and his eyes should be pretty much glued to you whenever you are together. How will you get that great attention? By free shaping it, of course. You have already laid the foundation for attention in your powering up the clicker exercise, now you just need to make sure you have that same attention everywhere you go, no matter what is going on.

Piggy Pointer

If my dog is "off duty" and I want him to start paying attention to me, I call his name. Because my dogs' names are the very happiest sound they know, they will immediately alert to me and start paying attention, because they know something exciting is coming up.

Notice that I am not prompting this dog for attention. I just wait for him to look at me and then I will click and treat him for it.

Seven Pillars of Listening
How to Teach Attention in Seven Steps

Step One

Begin at home with no distractions. Arm yourself with a bait pouch or a garment with big pockets filled with treats. Go about your regular business, but be alert to what your little friend is up to. Anytime your dog looks at you, click and treat. Begin by rewarding any slight glance. Your dog does not have to be near to you. As long as his head is turned in your direction, click it. By the end of the first day, you can start working up the duration of the stare. Work up to having him stare at you by using small approximations as you did when you played the box game. Wait one second before click and treat, then two seconds, then three, then four, and so forth. Do this for a few days and you will have a dog that bores holes into your head with his eyes.

Step Two

It is helpful to set up controlled situations to **proof** your dog's attention. By proof, I mean that he can continue to give you attention in a variety of situations. Start in the least stimulating environment where you are most likely to have good at-

54

tention—probably your kitchen. Pick one distraction and reward your dog for maintaining eye contact with you while the distraction is presented. Click and treat your dog for keeping his eyes on you as each distraction is presented. If he breaks position or loses attention, do not say or do anything. He will learn quickly enough that attention earns him rewards and everything else does not. Here is a sample of how you might add a progression of distractions:

Have a friend make a noise in another room.

Have a friend walk into the room.

Have a friend walk into the room and move towards your dog.

Have a friend walk into the room and move closer toward your dog.

Have a friend stand next to your dog.

Have a friend lean over your dog.

Have a friend hold her hand over your dog's shoulder.

Have a friend touch your dog's shoulder.

The smaller the progressive slices you reward, the faster and better your dog will learn. Change only one small thing at a time. You would never skip from a friend making noise in the other room to a friend leaning over your dog, because you would have changed at least three things—the physical presence of the friend, the closeness of the friend to your dog, and the friend leaning over your dog. The smaller the progressive slices you can reward, the better the behavior will be.

Click and treat for your dog maintaining eye contact when the distraction is presented. At first, even if your dog turns away to check out the noise/person, reinforce him when he looks back at you. Eventually, you want to hone that behavior down to steady eye contact. Gradually raise the criteria until a person is doing a jig and eating a hamburger right next to your dog and your dog is still staring at you. This is a very good way to teach your dog attention as a default behavior. Weird stuff = look at mom/dad.

Step Three

Now go out in your back yard with your dog on a 10 foot line. If you have a fence, just let your dog go. Walk around, tend to your business, and click/treat whenever your dog looks at you. You will be shocked at how quickly just going out into the yard becomes a cue for him to stare at you.

With the right training, distractions just become a cue for more attention. Ruby knows she will get cookies if she remains motionless regardless of what is happening around her.

Step Four

Finally, you are ready to take this behavior on the road. Begin in a fairly neutral area. The sidewalk in front of your house might be a good place to start. If space permits, use a ten foot lead and let your dog wander about. Click and treat any eye contact and build on it as outlined above. Move on to more and more exciting venues very gradually and only when you are getting very good attention in the less distracting setting.

Step Five

In this step, you will condition your dog so that "new environment" means "look at me." Simply being in a new place will become a cue to look at you. The problem with this is that new places are often just so darn stimulating that all of your lovely training cannot overcome the lure of the novel. Instead of giving you attention when he arrives at a new place, the first thing your dog might do is stand at the end of his leash, straining to get away and check out all that stuff. Remember, it is useless to give a command to a dog that is not paying attention to you.

So, what do you? Here is a game plan. Immediately discard all pride and stoop to the lowest level possible. Give your dog a huge wad of incredibly mouth-watering treats placed directly under his nose—shoved in his mouth, if necessary. Now, this looks for all appearances like a bribe, but it is actually much more than that. What you are really doing is conditioning your dog to pay attention to you when he enters a new environment. In this case, it does not matter what your dog is doing—we are just trying to set up an association between "new place" and "fabulous treats." Whenever you take a puppy (or untrained dog) somewhere new, you should always have a big wad of great treats in your hand when you enter the new building or location. As you open the door and allow the dog through, immediately stick your hand under his nose and shove treats in his mouth, before he has a chance to react to the new venue. If you do this enough times, whenever your dog goes somewhere new he will begin to drool and look at you expectantly, just like Pavlov's dog. Once you have your dog's attention this way, hesitate a split second before giving the next treat, and click him for maintaining eye contact during the hesitation. Then build on that hesitation until he is eagerly looking at you for a few seconds and then click that.

Once you have conditioned attention, you can go back to shaping the behavior you want. Now, instead of immediately feeding your dog every time he goes someplace new, you can hold out and wait for him to give you some attention. Click the attention and build it up to longer and longer duration, until your dog is trained to automatically check in with you whenever he is in a new place. It is a tricky thing to know when to switch from conditioning (giving the dog something for nothing, just to set up an association between being in a new place and getting treats) to training (expecting some attention from your dog and rewarding it). If your dog is responding to his name and appears able to pay attention to you, you can start training. If your dog's eyes still look like pinwheels and he is making desperate leaps at the end of his leash, you probably need to do more conditioning.

Here I am bringing a nine month old puppy into a training building full of other people and dogs. As we come through the door, I keep feeding him so he has no opportunity to look around. Once I have his attention in this way, I can go back to asking for all the behaviors he knows, like sit and loose leash walking.

Note that one is always walking a fine line when taking a not-so-completely-trained-dog or puppy to a new place. On one hand, you need to push the envelope so that your dog can be socialized, learn, and be conditioned to perform anywhere, but on the other hand you have to be very careful that your dog is capable of paying attention in a new place. You always need to set your dog up for success. If you find that your dog is completely out of control and unable to even take food from you when he gets to a new place, that is a pretty good indicator that you need to try a less stimulating environment.

Piggy Pointer
Don't be discouraged if you are all thumbs at first! You will get the hang of handling the leash, the treats, the door, the clicker, and the wildly lunging dog in no time. Don't be frustrated if you can't quite get it all together at first. Keep trying and you will become better able to manage multiple things while handling your dog.

Step Six

Gradually up the ante and take your dog to increasingly more and more stimulating environments. Start with an empty park, progress to a park with people in it, but start 100 yards away from where the people are. Gradually move closer, until you are working right in among the people. Once he is giving you attention with distractions, take him to the pet supply store, take him to the hardware store, obedience class, dog shows, agility trials, or anywhere else he is welcome.

Step Seven

Every minute you are with your dog, he is learning. If you want full attention from your dog, you have to give him full attention. There is no "down time" when you take your young or green dog to class or out on the road. Every second he is with you, you should be clicking and treating for attention. If you grow tired of this, put your dog away in a crate until you are prepared to once again give him your full attention. Whatever you do, don't ignore him while he is on leash with all that interesting stuff going on around him. He will definitely take the opportunity to self-reinforce, and you will not be happy with the results.

After reading the seven steps to attention, you may be thinking that all this attention stuff seems like a lot of work. Is it worth the effort? Why not give a command to a dog that is not paying attention to you? Might you not be able to convince him to pay attention to you by yelling the command louder? Let me tell you about a very interesting scientific study. Little electrodes were placed in a cat's ears to measure his hearing response. After taking a control sampling of the cat's hearing, a mouse in a cage was placed in front of the cat. Guess what? The cat could not hear when the mouse was present. The presence of the mouse was so stimulating that the cat's auditory centers literally shut down.

I know of no scientific study that proves it, but it is a safe assumption that dogs react to stimulation in the same way. When your dog gets to a new place and you call him and he fails to acknowledge you, he is not ignoring you, he is effectively deaf. Once again, the owner of the biddable dog has a head start on you. The basic functions that biddable dogs were bred for, like herding or retrieving, are inherently very stimulating activities. What makes a good working dog is a tremendous excitement and drive to carry out his work, but with the ability to stop on a dime and listen to his master's command, even from a great distance away. From my observation, it appears that many biddable dogs were bred to have an ability to keep listening, even when unbelievably aroused. It will come as no surprise to you that your Pigs Fly dog has no such pedigree.

Even in an exciting public place, Ruby automatically watches me and waits to be released each step of the way. Ruby was not born this way, but we built this lovely behavior over the years by rewarding her for each step again and again.

6

If You Can't Beat 'Em, Join 'Em

Using Your Dog's Natural Behaviors to Train Him

If you have started with the exercises in the previous chapters, you have a dog who is operant, and that is a very good start. He should be pretty enthusiastic about learning at this point. At least in your living room with no distractions, he appears to be more interested in training than anything else. Here's the problem. Your Pigs Fly dog still has a lot of passion in life to do things that are at odds with what you want him to do. Your dog is the dog who is obsessed by sniffing, who is oblivious to anything but running off to play with other dogs, or whose mind just checks out when he sees a flock of birds go up in the air. You could train a lot to overcome these distractions and eventually teach your dog "not" to sniff, play with other dogs, or chase fluttering things, but what a waste of great enthusiasm that would be. What if, instead of eliminating these behaviors, we could control them and use them as fuel to power the behaviors we want? What if we could find a way to make your dog as passionate about coming when called as he is about digging a hole? That is what we are going to do in this chapter.

Light a Fire With ICE
Capturing Your Dog's Interest

Let's call the things that have natural, pleasurable, meaning for your dog (like sniffing or chasing things) "hot" activities, and let's call the things that have no meaning for your dog (like heeling or coming when called) "cold" activities. By using the hot activities as reinforcers for the cold activities, the enthusiasm

Look at the focus and drive these Norwich Terriers have for digging.

that your dog feels for the original hot activity will, over time, transfer to the cold activity. The previously meaningless activity will take on the aura and excitement of the hot activity.

In order to get your Pigs Fly dog as on fire to lie down on cue as he is to chase squirrels, give him some **ICE!**

1. **I**dentify what your dog finds naturally motivating—his "hot" activities.

2. **C**ontrol the hot activities so that your dog can only get them from you, and

3. **E**xchange the chance for your dog to do a hot activity in return for your dog performing a cold activity

Live Wires
Identify Your Dog's Hot Reinforcers

The first step in making your dog excited to work with you is the "I" in ICE. Identify what your dog finds naturally motivating. Everything in dog training comes down to motivation, and motivation comes down to finding the reinforcer that your dog wants. The difficulty is, not all dogs want the same thing, and much of the things that a dog wants are distinctly incompatible with what you would like him to do. Isn't running away to play with other dogs, sniffing, or scurrying off to perform surgery on a stuffed toy incompatible with heeling with rapt attention? It may seem like the fact that your dog wants to chase squirrels is at odds with your desire to teach your dog to walk on a loose leash, but I am going to show you how they can really be one and the same desire.

When someone says that their dog lacks motivation or drive, what they are really saying is that their dog lacks motivation or drive to do the things that she, the handler, wants them to do. All dogs have motivation and drive, you just have to identify it. The first thing you need to do, therefore, is make a list of the things that your dog loves and has drive to do. Include everything, even destructive or "bad" things and we will sort them out later. I am going to talk about breed tendencies that I have observed that may give you some hints on where to look for reinforcers for your dog, but every dog is different and you should make no assumptions about what any individual dog loves to do. I recommend making a list of ten things and then prioritizing them.

Here are sample lists of hot reinforcers for three breeds of dog. Observe the differences and similarities. What it is most important to keep in mind is that these are hot reinforcers, meaning that they are things that the dogs loved to do before they were trained or conditioned to do so. Lots of dogs love things like doing agility, playing retrieve games, or getting praise from their handlers, but very few were born loving those things. We need to know what our dogs' hot reinforcers are because those are the things that we can use motivate them to do the things that we want them to do.

Cherry - Bull Terrier (A particularly un-biddable breed in the Terrier Group)

1. Ball (playing with it on her own)

2. Playing with other dogs

3. Attacking sprayed water

4. Chasing cats/deer/anything that moves

5. Food

6. Chasing handler

7. Being shoved and "roughed up" by handler

8. Swimming

9. Sniffing around

10. Affection/patting/praise from handler

Here is the anatomy of an un-biddable dog: predictably for a Terrier, much of what she finds extremely reinforcing are ritualized chasing and hunting games. The ball mimics the actions of a prey animal, and playing with other dogs is to some degree an extension of hunting activity. Notice that affection from her handler is way down on the list—a dismal last, in fact. Also note that almost all of the activities that she loves do not involve her handler in any way. If you feel despair when you read this list because it resembles your own dog's list, please note that this was my dog and, after she was trained, she would go anywhere with me, do whatever I asked, and would never take her eyes off of me for fear of missing something fun.

Beau - Border Collie (Among the most biddable of breeds in the Herding Group)

1. Herding/chasing sheep

2. Retrieving games (Frisbee™, ball, any other toy)

3. Chasing a ball.

4. Tug games with handler

5. Chase/pounce games with handler

6. Swimming

7. Handler praise

8. Food rewards

9. Going for a walk

10. Physical affection from handler

Here is a biddable dog. Border Collies are generally perceived to be the most easily trained dogs of all. He loves toys, too, but he loves playing with his handler and the toy. The Terrier had three activities involving her handler, and they were all in the bottom half of her priorities. Six out of ten of the Border Collie's hot activities involve his handler, and three of the top five are handler games!

This Rhodesian Ridgeback is obviously not in love with doing an obedience exercise, but it does not mean that he lacks drive. Just look at him lure coursing (chasing a plastic bag on a string that simulates a rabbit running through a large field). That is the drive you want to harness and use.

Mr. Bailey - Rhodesian Ridgeback (A fairly unbiddable breed from the Hound Group)

1. Lure Coursing

2. Chasing Squirrels

3. Running free

4. Chase games with handler

5. Hide and seek games with handler

6. Walks

7. Food

8. Being near handler

9. Sniffing/tracking things

10. Handler talking to him/getting attention

What a surprise, four out of the top five for this dog involve some kind of chasing and hunting behavior. Although he values his freedom, interaction with his handler is still high on his list and he has a strong desire to be with and play with his handler. This is a dog that is not going to be as hard to train as the Bull Terrier, but the things he loves best do not involve his handler and it will be still be a challenge to motivate him.

Pig-tionary
Lure Coursing: "Coursing" is the pursuit of game by sight as opposed to scent. Dogs who hunt this way are called sighthounds. Lure coursing is a sport where the action of prey is simulated by a plastic bag tied to a cord which is stretched around pulleys in a field. The cord is run by a motor which whips the bag around a course with several turns, anywhere from 600 to 1000 yards long.

Now make your own list. Write down ten of your dog's "hot" activities. Remember, even jumping up on you or lunging at squirrels counts. Even though they are not things we like our dogs to do, it will tell us what we need to know about what motivates our dogs. Think carefully about your dog and for what things he shows a lot of enthusiasm. A lot of people have trouble motivating their dogs because they are confused about what motivates their dogs. The assumption is often made, for instance, that praise and petting are hot reinforcers. In fact, most dogs (especially Pigs Fly kind of dogs) don't care a fig about petting and praise to start out with. It is only as you painstakingly develop your relationship with your dog over months or even years that your dog comes to find your approval rewarding—you have to earn the privilege of being reinforcing to your dog!

Pig Tale
It is the very rare dog that is in good health and not motivated by food. A lot of people tell me that their dogs are not motivated by food, but it is almost never true. I brought my 11 month old Bull Terrier puppy to a group training class. I knew this was going to be distracting and stimulating enough to blow the top of

his head off, so I pulled out the heavy artillery. I bought a loin of pork (on sale) and roasted it with paprika and garlic salt. It was unbelievably delicious and I had a few pieces myself. I was loaded for bear and ready for class.

At class, there was a very nice woman just starting with her first dog and we began chatting. I noticed that her dog had an attention problem, and she was only using dry dog biscuits as a reinforcer. I offered to give her some of my pork loin to help get her dog working, but she told me that her dog was not motivated by treats. About 15 minutes later it was time for off-leash work. The second she took the leash off, her dog bee-lined for my bag on the other side of the arena (he had bookmarked the location, apparently), and dove his entire head right into my bucket of treats. He looked pretty motivated, to me. If you think your dog is not motivated by food, you probably need to improve your cooking.

Have you made your list? What is at the top? If your dog has a very strong desire to do anything at all, you will have an easy time training him. I promise you, even if your dog has a very strong desire to run crazy laps and ignore you completely, you are in good shape. It is the really naughty dogs that are easy to train. If your dog is active and cares deeply about getting reinforcements, be it a toy, food, or the environment in general, it is a cinch to transfer that passion to another (desirable) activity. I love it when a new student shows up with a wild, lunging dog. If the dog jumps on me and tries to lick, paw, or gently gnaw me, better yet. We can take that energy and channel it into whatever behavior we want, picking up good manners on the way. If, however, your dog's top reinforcers are:

1. Lying on the couch,

2. Lying on the bed,

3. Lying on the deck,

4. Lying under the table,

and so forth, you have a more complex task to tackle. You cannot train an inert lump to do anything. You are going to have to teach him how to desire things. My first recommendation is that you honestly assess your dog's weight and put him on a diet (ask your veterinarian for guidance). He should have plenty of ribs showing. Being just a tiny bit hungry is very motivating (and extremely healthy). Next, pay attention to Chapter Seven, where we discuss how to teach your dog to play, and work a lot on free shaping games. Over time, you will find your dog perking up and beginning to care about things.

The Keeper of the Keys
Control of Reinforcers

Now that you have a list of your dog's hot reinforcers, you are going to work on the "C" in ICE. Control the hot activities so that your dog can only get them from you. Think of those hot reinforcers as cash. Imagine you walk into a bank and money is just lying around all over the place with a big sign "Free for the Taking." When you walked into that bank, would you stand on line and wait to use a cash machine to take money out of your own account? Of course not. You would just pick up the cash on the floor. If, on the other hand, the only way you could get money was to wait in line, put your debit card in the cash machine, punch some buttons, and then get cash from your account, you would readily perform those behaviors because you have no option. What we want to do is pick up all that "money" that is lying around in your dog's world, and put it into the cash machine that you control—you! The hot reinforcers are the cash, and you are the cash machine. The dog has to punch the correct buttons to get some money.

Some reinforcers, like food and toys, are easy to control because you can take physical control of them. If your dog has a toy or ball fetish, you are very lucky. I have had two dogs in my life that were ball-obsessed and all I had to do was say, "Want your ballie?" and I had their complete attention. The key here is to never allow your dog to have that valuable toy except in exchange for a behavior. It is also very helpful to have a cue for that toy, for example, "Want Your Ballie?" "Where's Your Toy?" "Get Your Frisbee." The cue is easy enough to teach, because the toy resonates so deeply with these kinds of dogs. Just pairing the cue with the toy a few times is usually all it takes.

Where things get more complicated is when your dog's hot reinforcers are things like sniffing or running around. These are things that you cannot easily control, so you need to take the time to put them on cue. Sniffing in particular is an activity that brings dog trainers much grief, but is invaluable as a reinforcer when put on cue. All dogs enjoy sniffing to a greater or lesser degree, and it is very good to have sniffing available as a **life reward**—a reward you can have with you and use any time, anywhere. If you have a scent hound, putting sniffing on cue should be your first order of business.

Here is one way to put sniffing on cue. Take your dog somewhere where you know he will be likely to want to sniff. Shorten up on your leash so he does not have a lot of freedom, but do not use the leash to pull him or prompt him in any way. The leash is only a barrier to manage control your dog's access to sniffing, not a training tool. Wait until he looks at you, and then say "Go sniff" and release the leash so he can put his head down and sniff. If your dog really likes to sniff, it should not take long for him to catch on to this fun game. Eventually, any time you say, "Go sniff" your dog will happily oblige. Let's call this the "release" method of teaching a cue to sniff. The nice thing about teaching it this way is that not only are you getting an important behavior on cue, but you are exchanging something you want (attention) for something he wants (sniffing) and that will strengthen the behavior of paying attention to you. However, teaching the sniff cue this way has its drawbacks, as I will describe in the next paragraph.

Here is the reward for that great healing—go sniff!

Alternatively, you could just capture the sniffing behavior and use a clicker to mark it. Wait until your dog is sniffing, then click and treat. As soon as he puts his head down to sniff again, click and treat. If you have been playing your free shaping games, your dog will quickly figure out that he can offer the behavior of sniffing for a treat. Once he is obviously offering the behavior, add a cue like "Go sniff" just as his head is lowering to the ground to sniff. This method will isolate the behavior more quickly and make it much clearer to the dog exactly what the cue means than does the "release" method. If you just generally release the dog and allow him to sniff as in the previous paragraph, the dog might think that "go sniff" means "do whatever you want to do." It so happens that, for the heavy sniffers, "whatever you want to do" generally means sniffing. However, it might also mean walk away, eat some dirt, bark at another dog, or jump on you. You may not know for a long time that you have not actually trained a "sniff" command because "sniff" is the default behavior of many dogs. However, that day may come when you say "Go sniff" and your dog simply walks away from you because he thinks he can do whatever he wants, which happens not to be sniffing on that particular day. If you have a dog that finds sniffing very reinforcing, you want to have precise control over that behavior, so I would always use some capturing of the behavior to be sure that the dog really understands the cue. Both the "release" and "capture" methods are handy in different contexts and both can, if correctly used, strengthen the "sniff" cue.

Be creative about your reinforcers and, if your dog gets really excited about something, try to find a way to incorporate it into your training sessions. I keep a kiddie pool just outside my training yard. I have a couple of students whose dogs just live to go swimming and, after a particularly good sequence, the dog is released to "go swimming!" The entire training session is now infused with the delicious possibility that swimming may just be around the corner.

The opportunity to get in the water is an overwhelmingly powerful draw for a Newfoundland. Because he knows he can earn the opportunity to swim by doing behaviors that his owner wants, the water has ceased to be a distraction and has become a motivator instead.

When we put behaviors that a dog likes (such as sniffing or swimming) on cue, we can have them available as rewards to offer our dogs for behaviors we like (such as walking on a loose leash, coming when called, or lying down.) That is all very well and good, but what is to keep the dog from doing those reinforcing activities whenever he darn well pleases? Why should he wait to be invited by you? In short, how do you gain control over those fun behaviors so that your dog can only do them if you say so? Well, there is a beautiful side effect to putting "incompatible with working" activities on cue. Once a dog has a behavior on cue, he will tend to offer it only when cued to do so. It doesn't seem possible, but it is a well-known fact and almost always is true. If your dog keeps indulging in a behavior that is interfering with the training process (like sniffing, zooming around, or jumping up in the air and barking at squirrels), get those behaviors on cue and give your dogs lots of opportunities to do them when it is convenient for you. You will be amazed at how quickly the "problem" behaviors disappear.

It's a Toll Road, Not a Barricade
Give Your Dog Access to What He Loves

Here is a key concept in the Pigs Fly system. In order to be successful at controlling reinforcers, in order for this system to work at all, you must make sure that your dog has a reasonable opportunity to access those reinforcers. You have to be a gatekeeper, not a blocker. Ponder for a moment your image of a gatekeeper versus a blocker. A gatekeeper is someone who allows you to pass through the gate to get to where you very much want to go. On the other hand, a blocker is someone who is, at all costs, going to foil your attempts to get where you want to go. Don't you just hate people like that? Your dog does, too. If there is a reasonable way to get past the gatekeeper, by paying a toll for instance, you will do so. It is an easy and fair system. If, instead, a blocker has shut down the road entirely and is vigilantly guarding the gate to keep you from passing, you are going to put a lot of effort into finding an alternate route. That is to say, if you never give your dog an opportunity to earn a sniffing, digging, running, or shredding a stuffed toy session, your dog is going to put his energy into getting around you to do those things and, trust me, he has almost unlimited energy for figuring out how to get around you. He will dart off the instant you are not micro-managing him, sneak in the forbidden behavior, and it will really tick you off. If, however, your dog knows that doing some nice loose leash walking might earn him an opportunity to sniff, dig, run around, or perform a squeak-ectomy on a stuffed toy, he will put his energy into loose leash walking.

So, in so far as possible, everything that your dog loves needs to be physically controlled by you, and/or put on cue. In addition, you need to restrict your dog's ability to self-reinforce. How much management is necessary to do this will all depend on what reinforcers you are using and where your dog is in his training program. For instance, most of my dogs find balls, squeaky toys, and stuffed toys highly valuable. Those toys are only available to them when we are training. They have other toys that are available to them all the time so that they can play casually with me or among themselves, but the most enticing toys are reserved for training.

When we are talking about behaviors as opposed to food or toys, the situation becomes more complicated, because you can't carry "sniffing" or "running around" in your pocket. You need to make sure that, when you take your dog out for a training session, he is not self reinforcing by sniffing, play-lunging at other dogs, eating poop, digging a hole, or whatever else he finds interesting. That means that you do what you have to do to make his world small enough you control everything. You should never correct or in any way punish your dog for doing something you do not want him to do—just don't give him the opportunity to do it. Until you have reliable attention from your dog and his hot activities are on cue and under your control, the easiest solution is either to physically restrict your dog from activities until you release him (work him on a leash or long line), or to find a place to train that is boring and familiar (like your kitchen).

If you find yourself in a situation where your dog is getting a lot of self reinforcement just by virtue of being in a particular place and he has no interest in working with you, give him some crate time until he calms down. If that does not work, try going back to your vehicle (assuming you drove to wherever you are) and working on attention there. If that doesn't work, you probably need to take things back a step and go to a less stimulating environment. Likewise, avoid constant praise, patting, or even just fussy interaction ("herefidoherefidohereherelookhere-looklook") when the dog is not offering a behavior you like. Sometimes simply being in public and having the opportunity to ignore you is really fun for your dog—this is not a pleasure to which you want to introduce him.

Allow me to note here that it is barbaric and cruel to withhold all meaningful social contact from a dog unless the dog is working for you. Likewise, never allowing a hound to go out in the back yard and sniff, a terrier to go out in the back yard and dig, or a northern breed to frolic in the snow would stunt normal development and intelligence of the animal. Yes, you have to be the key to everything fun and good for your dog. However, totally isolating your dog and only allowing interaction with you and not other people or dogs is not a good or humane plan. The more experiences and positive interactions your dog has with other dogs, people, and environments, the more intelligent and well-adjusted he will be. Remember, we are talking about control of resources, not deprivation of resources! It is a delicate balance, but you have to make sure your dog has lots of "just be a dog" time, as well as time where he is restricted in what he can do and has to offer you behaviors to get permission to do things he wants to do.

Pig Tale

One of my dogs, Ruby, is almost unbelievably willful and smart. This also means she is a big pain in the rear to live with. If it can be scratched or chewed, she will figure out how get to it and complete her mission of destruction. Because of these qualities, she gets very little "free" time in the house. Even at four years of age, she cannot be trusted without supervision. She gets just as much free time in the house as the other dogs, but I have shaped her to always be at my side and always offering behaviors. Although she does have increasingly long intervals of calmly lying around (which I reinforce heavily), I still have to keep her with me most of the time. It is a big responsibility and tiresome at times to have a dog that shadows you, offering behaviors, but it is better than the unpleasant behaviors with which she will amuse herself if left unattended. Ruby's seven month old puppy, on the other hand, is trustworthy and calm around the house and is allowed almost complete freedom when loose inside. You have to adjust your training plan to the dog.

A Fair Exchange
A Hot Activity in Return for a Cold Activity

Now that you know what your dog loves to do, and you have gotten control over those activities and things, you are ready to move on to the "E" in ICE—exchange the chance for your dog to do a hot activity in return for your dog performing a cold activity. You will give him access to those activities and things he naturally loves in exchange for doing something that you want him to do. This will accomplish two goals. First, your dog will learn to take it as a truth in life that if he wants something, he can get it if he does something for you. That alone will greatly improve your relationship with your dog and make your life easier. Second, if you pair a hot activity, like chasing a ball, with a cold activity, like walking on a loose leash, you can condition your dog to feel just as good about walking on a loose leash as he does about chasing balls. Thus you are changing your dog's behavior on two levels:

1. You are training him to think about how to do things that please you (and cause you give to him reinforcers); and

2. You are conditioning him to have a general feeling of happiness and excitement about doing things that you want him to do. Furthermore, you will be conditioning him to have a feeling of happiness and excitement about you in general, since you are the gateway to everything he loves.

In Chapter Nine, you will use hot activities to teach basic foundation behaviors. For now, just understand how and why it is important to identify, control, and use hot reinforcers.

Terriers generally prefer to be on their feet and busy rather than lying down and waiting. With a ball as a reinforcer, however, Nicky will plant himself on the ground next to me.

Bringing the Mountain to Mohammed
Getting in Front of Your Dog

When I was struggling with training my first Bull Terrier, I kept reading and hearing that I had to find out what was motivating to my dog and keep my training sessions fun. While there is nothing wrong with this advice, it is not particularly helpful, either. It is more a statement of the problem than the solution to the problem. You certainly do have to find out what motivates your dog, and training has to be fun, but how do you achieve that goal? The secret, and the thing that few people seem to understand when dealing with a non-biddable dog, is that you have to become your dog's main motivation. That is why it is so easy to train some dogs—being with their handler is their primary motivation. You can shape your Pigs Fly dog to be the same way as those biddable dogs by conditioning him to equate you with all the things in life that he loves. To do this, follow the three rules of motivation: identify the things that your dog loves, then gain control of them, and then exchange them on a regular basis for behaviors that you want. If you can do that, you will have your dog's undivided attention and just being with you will be his idea of a great time.

In addition, you need to scrupulously ignore any behaviors that you do not want. You especially have to avoid any corrections, even very mild verbal reprimands, such as "eh, eh." Why? Because nagging corrections of this kind are simply indications to your dog that he is free to ignore you until you notice him. He does not have to solicit your attention, because he knows you will be working to get his attention. Remember this—although you are the primate with the big brain and the opposable thumbs, you have a lot on your mind. You have to get ready for work, you have to make your children's lunch, you have to mow your lawn, you volunteered to work the local recycling center this Saturday, and forgot that you already promised to pick up your mother at the airport. Darn! You forgot to buy milk again! Your dog, on the other hand, has a much clearer agenda—his life is about equally divided into sleeping and getting you to do what he wants. You may not see this at first, but if you take a long view you will see that your dog probably has done a really great job of training you while you were thinking about other stuff.

Let's say you are moving about your house, busy doing things. Suddenly, you become aware that your dog has your best underwear in his mouth and he is brandishing it with great relish. You run after him, take the item away from him and scold him. Your dog is thinking something along the lines of, "Score! Now I know how to get her attention!" Your dog has trained you to run after him and give him a fun game of chase. Say instead that you are out for a walk and you ask your dog to sit. He ignores you. You ask again, he ignores you again and looks away. You say "look-look-look-watch-watch-watch" and you dog maybe turns an ear in your direction. Finally, you produce a cookie out of your pocket and put it in front of his nose and lure him into a sit. The bubble above your dog's head reads, "Success! I have trained her to produce cookies for the simplest of behaviors! I never need to pay attention, because I know I don't have to do anything unless that reward is present."

If you just dole out rewards as a bribe when your dog is misbehaving or not paying attention in order to lure him back to you, that puts the dog squarely in the driver's seat—he can just cruise along and do his own thing until you notify him that his next goodie is ready. That puts you Behind Your Dog. Likewise, if you always initiate a session by showing a dog the reinforcer, and then use it to lure the dog around, you may get the behavior you want. But your dog will only have learned to follow a lure, he will not have learned that he needs to keep his eye on you. Instead, your dog needs to understand that: 1) you will be ignoring any undesirable behaviors, including the behavior of not paying attention to you; and 2) he has to come to you and solicit rewards by offering behaviors. This is what I call Getting In Front Of Your Dog.

Piggy Pointer

If you are In Front Of Your Dog, you do not need a specific command for attention—just being with you is a cue for your dog to pay attention. And if you give your dog a cue for some behavior and he does not respond, do not repeat the cue. Wait at least ten seconds and try again. If your dog still does not respond, you probably need to do more training for the cue in that context.

Getting In Front Of Your Dog all comes down to timing and management. For instance, if you know you will be busy around the house, and you know your dog might get into mischief, put your dog in a crate for a while. Or keep him with you and reinforce him often for just hanging out quietly with you. Train when you can, and if you can't train, manage the situation so the dog will not do anything wrong. If your dog does not sit and/or pay attention to you the first time you ask, the lunch counter is closed and he missed his opportunity to get a treat. It takes a little thought at first, but eventually it will be second nature to set up your dog so he is always doing the right thing.

Lots of people interpret a "fun" training session as one where they continually speak to their dog in a high, squeaky voice, and dance around in a "fun" manner. Many dogs are actually backed off by this kind of behavior—motivational does not mean "nice," motivational means that which motivates a particular dog. Dogs tend to be drawn into a composed handler with a soft smile. If your dog is shy or reluctant, cheerleading-style handling will actually make the problem worse. General silly behavior makes you look positive and motivational to other humans, but it is, at best, just white noise to your dog. You want to have a squeaky voice or a crazy dance in your basket of reinforcers (I certainly do), but assuming a generally goofy persona is not communicating anything to your dog. In fact, if you are constantly streaming meaningless praise and cheerleading your dog in the hope that he will be encouraged to do what you want, you will have ruined one of the best and handiest reinforcers you have available. Your dog won't care about praise and attention anymore because he gets them all the time for no reason. Even worse, although you think you are "encouraging" your dog to follow along with your plans, you might actually reinforce your dog's non-responsive behavior.

Make no mistake, praise and exciting "happy" sounds are reinforcers—you want to give you dog plenty of them, but after he has done something for you, not before. Your goal is to have an aura as still and large as a mountain beneath which all the doggie treasures of the world are buried. A mountain doesn't leap about and squeak, but somehow it is there in your field of vision. It is always in front of you. That is how you need to be to your dog.

Just finding out what motivates your dog and using those things in your training sessions to infuse behaviors with excitement is a piece of the puzzle, but Getting In Front of Your Dog is the next level, and the one that makes everything work. Sure, you could get most behaviors with a lure or by nagging your dog for attention, but, that is way too much work for me. As much as it seems like I have unlimited energy for training, I have a side that is, if not lazy, always looking for the most efficient way to do things. I'd rather have my little friend working to please me rather than the other way around, wouldn't you?

This little dog enjoys a chin rub as a reinforcer.

7

Play University

Learning How to Play With Your Dog

At this point you have laid in a good foundation to train a variety of behaviors. If your dog's list of "hot" reinforcers includes lots of games and play with you, you probably are in pretty good shape. If play is not on your dog's list of hot reinforcers, you have some more work to do. Being able to use play as a reinforcer is essential if you want reliability and consistency from your dog, anywhere, anytime.

First Things First
Why Play Comes Before Work in Dog Training

Let's take the example of teaching a dog to walk on a loose leash. If your dog enjoys tugging on a rope toy, you have a motivator that is small and light enough to carry around with you. You can inject some excitement into walking with you by breaking out the toy and playing tug with it from time to time. Sometimes you can just show the rope toy and run or jump around a little or speak in an excited voice. Ultimately, you would like him to get so fired up on just the possibility of playing, that he charges after you wherever you go whether armed with the tug toy or not. The "finished product" motivator is walking around with you, with the possibility of a wild and crazy play session breaking out at any moment. You are the only motivator you will have on you all the time, and the chance for a fun time with you can be the best motivator for keeping your dog's attention and getting a happy performance.

Now, think about a dog whose only motivator is food. How far is that going to get you? You will have a dog that works readily and eagerly for the food, but is cut adrift when the treats are not forthcoming. You have a dog that does three or four steps of walking, and then starts looking for a treat, then takes two more steps looking for a treat after each one, and then takes one more and stops, because he has no idea what he is doing "wrong." The operant dog looks for reinforcers as confirmation that he is doing the right thing. If a reinforcer is not forthcoming, he assumes he is doing something "wrong." If your dog's only reinforcer is food, he assumes he is wrong if he is not getting a treat. If, on the other hand, you have a dog who finds playing with you reinforcing, the mere fact that you are continuing to move around and whoop like an idiot from time to time is totally reinforcing and the dog knows he is right.

See how play can turn a routine activity, like walking down the driveway on leash, into an exciting one? After a little play, I become much more interesting and he can't take his eyes off of me.

The operant dog looks for reinforcers as confirmation that he is doing the right thing. If a reinforcer is not forthcoming, he assumes he is doing something "wrong."

Think about this statement carefully, for it is of profound significance. The absence of reinforcement is actually punishment to an operant dog. In contrast, a dog that has been trained to heel by using leash checks thinks he is in good shape so long as he is not getting leash checks. The understanding between the handler and the dog is that, if the handler is not tugging on the leash, the dog is performing correctly. Now, if you are following the Pigs Fly system, your non-biddable dog will be offering behaviors looking for a reward. He will be trotting along at your side, trying out different things to get that clicker to go off. Depending on where you are in your training and your dog's level of persistence, your dog may offer two steps, three steps or twenty steps and then, when he does not get a treat, he will stop and look at you as if to say, "What's up? What am I doing wrong? Why aren't you reinforcing me?" In short, he will give up. This is why it is so crucial that your dog comes to perceive the entire training process as a potential for all kinds of unexpected and exciting reinforcements—not just food. We must scientifically build an ongoing state of excited anticipation that will keep your dog on the hook and vibrating with eagerness to see what you will do next.

Piggy Pointer
People often feel annoyed or offended when their dog trembles with willingness to do their bidding in the presence of food, and then completely loses interest in the absence of food. The incorrect conclusion that people draw is that they should not use food to train, because then the dog only wants to work for food. On the contrary, food is a great motivator for all the reasons I have listed above. However, once your dog has learned how to perform behaviors, you need to move past food on to other reinforcers and vary the reinforcers so that the dog is in a constant, excited, state of happy anticipation. It is the incorrect application of the food motivator that is the problem, not the food itself.

The other problem with using only food is that you need to vary your reinforcement types to keep your dog excited and engaged in the task at hand. You may notice that, after a while, your dog starts not responding to your cues, or responds in a slow, lackluster manner. That is because he knows exactly what he is going to get in exchange for the behavior, so why rush? Your dog may like some kind of reinforcers more than others, but varying the reinforcement types will keep your dog on the hook much better than if you just used the dog's hottest reinforcer alone. This is the science behind the casino industry. Imagine you are playing a slot machine. You put in a nickel, and you get back two nickels, every time. You would probably sit there for a long time, since you are winning, but it's not terribly exciting. After a while, it will even begin to seem like drudgery, as if you are at work. Basically, you are getting paid by the hour to pull a lever again and again, and that is boring! Now imagine that you put in a nickel, and get nothing, but there is a possibility, however remote, that you might get $1,000,000. On some pulls of the lever you get two nickels, sometimes none, sometimes 100, but there is always that jackpot possibility out there. The fact that you are actually losing money over time is not relevant—every pull of that lever makes your heart race a little because you are excited by the possibilities and you are having fun.

That is where you need to be with your dog. Your dog pulls the slot handle by doing a behavior. Lemon, lemon, apple—he gets a cheese ball. Apple, apple, apple—he gets to chase a Frisbee. Lemon, lime, pineapple—he gets two cheese balls. Pineapple, Pineapple, Pineapple—HOLY COW! He gets to shred a stuffed toy into tiny pieces!!!! YAY!

Based on the first part of this chapter, you may be wondering if using food is a good idea, at all. Let me assure you, food is an irreplaceable tool and I am in no way suggesting that you should not use food. I just want you to understand when and why you need other kinds of reinforcers, too. Food is generally the very best reinforcer for initially teaching behaviors and one should not be in a hurry to get away from using it. Food has a particularly salient effect on the dog and the trainer can get the most mileage out of it as a reinforcer because of the precision with which it can be doled out and positioned. Furthermore, food actually puts a dog's brain in a good place for learning. Food stimulates the parasympathetic nervous system—generally a calming sensation. When we use food in training, we are actually helping to keep our dogs' minds in the calm, thinking part of the brain, instead of the wild, reflexive part of the brain. This helps your dog to learn new and complicated tasks more easily. However, for all the reasons listed above, you will need other kinds of reinforcers for your dog to progress in his training program. Besides that, playing is fun, and anything fun you do with your dog is like putting money into a "relationship bank."

We Are Not Leaving Until You Have Fun
Convincing Your Dog it's Fun to Play

Every dog knew how to play when he was a puppy—some of them just have forgotten how. Your job is to remind them how to play, and to let them know that it's OK to play with you. Not surprisingly, many biddable dogs have very high energy and a strong desire for play, especially for games that involve handler interaction, like fetch and tugging. That is very handy because, once again, it means a biddable dog's main reinforcement is, to some degree, his handler. Your Pigs Fly dog might not care about toys or playing with you. You need to teach him to value those things so that you can put yourself in the center of his universe.

Let's begin with that most basic of canine games, chasing a ball. I don't know why, but lots of dogs go crazy for the magic orb. If your dog already loves chasing balls, be sure to spend a few minutes each day playing this game with him. Throwing a ball is nice light exercise for people of all ages and a great bonding activity to do with your dog. It is a wonderful thing that your dog can only get through you, and that increases your dog's interest in you!

If you dog does not appear to like chasing a ball, try different types and sizes of balls. My dog Ursa is completely unmoved by a tennis or similarly sized ball, but will go insane for anything around the size of a soccer ball or larger. Literally, I cannot let her have a large ball because she will charge around the yard with it until the skin on her nose is bleeding and she is about to drop from exhaustion. Nicky is lukewarm to a hard rubber ball, but loves tennis balls so much that he becomes unhinged at even the smell of one. If there is a ¼ inch square of tennis ball material anywhere in a one acre enclosure, he will find it, pick it up, and stagger around in a fit of tennis ball-induced ecstasy. Cherry was equally enchanted by anything round regardless of the material it was made of, but it had to be small enough for her to pick it up. Experiment with different balls and see if any of them appeal to your dog.

Have you tried every single ball on the market already? When you throw the ball, does your dog still completely ignore it or look at you with a bubble above his head that says, "These humans are so strange. Why did she do that?" Here is how you can teach your dog to love playing with a ball.

1. Take a ball out and throw it in the back yard, then madly dash over to where it is and pick it up yourself. Just the fact that you have broken into a run is an attention getter, and your dog will probably stand there with a quizzical look on his face. This is a start—at least your dog will have noticed that Something Is Happening. If your physique does not permit a "mad dash," any gait that is above your normal speed will pique your dog's interest. Don't invite your dog to join in the game, just run after the ball, pick it up, toss it in the air a couple of times while speaking nonsense in an excited voice, and throw it again. This is the point where you will be thankful for privacy fencing, because otherwise your neighbors will have their hands poised over their telephones, wondering if it is time finally to call and have you committed.

2. Usually somewhere in the first week, your dog will begin to trot after you as you run to get the ball. Eventually, your dog will work up to dashing off with you to get the ball. You may have to throw that ball for days, or even weeks, before your dog starts getting excited, but don't get discouraged. Make sure

you get to the ball first, pick it up like a hot potato, toss it from hand to hand like it's burning your fingers, and then "accidentally" drop it so your dog can get it. Don't offer it or try to get your dog to interact with it in any way. It's that sense of snatching it from you that really lights up a dog. If your dog does not immediately leap on the ball when you drop it, quickly grab it and run off with it. It will not take long after that for your dog to start running after it himself.

3. Do not try to get your dog to bring the ball back to you. Just go and pick it up wherever your dog drops it and throw it again. Your dog will naturally begin bringing it back to you over time, and you will have a great game.

All of Ruby's enthusiasm and joy for chasing a ball is the result of training and practice. You can teach your dog to enjoy playing!

My dog, Ruby, had no interest in the ball, and less interest in running anywhere quickly. She rarely broke out of a trot when she was around me. Now she trembles with excitement when I pick up a ball, and will gladly perform any behavior in exchange for the opportunity to chase it. It took many weeks before she got the hang of the game, and many months, if not years, before she became a ball maniac, but it did happen. Don't give up if your dog takes a really long time to pick up on how much fun it is to chase a ball and don't be in a hurry.

Piggy Pointer

It does not matter if your dog does not bring the ball back to you. The entire point of this game is that your dog thinks it is great to chase after the ball. You can use that as a reinforcer to get other behaviors that you would like your dog to do. So what if you have to walk over and pick up the ball to throw it again? Most of us need the exercise, anyway. If you want to teach your dog to retrieve, you can do that separately, but the point of this exercise is to build another reinforcer for your dog, not to teach him to retrieve.

It is also helpful if, when you are first teaching this game, you play it at the same time each day. Even if the game only creates the tiniest bit of excitement at first, you can quickly condition your dog to anticipate that excitement at a certain time of day and that will help build more excitement. For instance, when some people come home from work the first thing they do is take their dog outside and throw the ball a few times. This is great because it is coupling the excitement of coming home with the ball playing game. You can condition a lot of interest into the ball very quickly that way. If you are lucky enough to have another person willing to help you, you can run after the ball together, tussle for it, toss it to each other, and generally act very excited about the ball. Watching other people play this game seems to make dogs understand the fun of it very quickly.

Experiment with throwing different things. Some dogs go crazy for Frisbee type toys. Squeaky toys are excellent attention getters. If you squeeze all the air out of the squeaky toy before you throw it, it will make a hideous wailing noise as it sails through the air. Many dogs find that noise irresistible. If food is your dog's top motivator, throw a bait bag full of food. Give your dog some of the food after he picks up the bag—there's no need for him to bring it back to you, but jackpot him if he does.

A Win-Win Situation

Tug Games

When it comes to pure, interactive fun, nothing beats a tug game. Getting a reluctant dog interested in tugging can be a challenge, but if you consider your dog's breed characteristics and adapt your play style accordingly, you will succeed. Generally, dragging a toy on the ground is more enticing than shoving it in your dog's face. The more you can imitate the scurrying movement of a rodent, the more interesting the toy will be. Likewise, standing at an oblique angle to your dog while you brandish your toy is more fun for your dog than if you stand over him. Some hardy breeds will enjoy being shoved around a bit while you initiate the game, particularly if you push them away in the chest as you run off with the toy. With toy-sized dogs or dogs with a soft temperament, I crouch so that I am actually facing slightly away from them and gently drag the toy along the ground. Especially with little dogs, you should let the dog do the tugging and you just hold the toy. If you tug too hard you can hurt your small dog's neck and back.

Piggy Pointer

If your dog is fearful, reactive, or aggressive, consult a professional trainer before trying any kind of rough play with your dog, including tug games. For normal dogs, these games do not in any way present an increased risk of aggression. On the contrary, teaching a dog to play within bounds strengthens his bond with you and teaches him how to feel free and comfortable with you. However, for less mentally stable dogs, play can actually be threatening and is best built up to under professional supervision.

Try to pick a tug toy that will play on your dog's hot reinforcers. A birdy dog might like something that flutters as you pull it along. A terrier might like something with a vermin-like squeak to it. A ball-crazy Dalmatian might appreciate a rope toy that has a tennis ball attached to it. Use your imagination and come up with a toy that has some natural appeal for your dog.

If you dog cannot be enticed to tug no matter how attractive you make it for him, you can easily clicker train a dog to love tugging. Tugging is a good example of a cold reinforcer that can quickly become a hot reinforcer. Simply approximate the tug—dog touches tug toy, dog puts mouth on tug toy, dog holds tug toy with your hand on it, dog holds toy as you pull gently on it, etc.

Big dogs and Terriers often like to be shoved in the chest when playing. Face-on rough play, with lots of growling and shoving can be very appealing to large or hardy dogs.

Another great way to convince your dog that it's fun to tug is to use a tug toy that holds food, such as the Tug-N-Treat™. The Tug-N-Treat is a heavy nylon pouch with a handle and Velcro closure. You can place great treats in the pouch, show your dog what is in there, close it up, and present it to him. He will almost certainly take it in his mouth and try to get to the food inside, and you can begin your tugging game.

Small dogs tend to feel less inhibited if you hold your body at an angle to them while playing. Many small dogs find face-on tug games to be intimidating.

If you teach your dog to tug, you also need to teach him to release the toy on cue. Take your dog by the collar and let go of the toy. That immediately stops the fun, and keeps your dog from running off. Do not choke, shake, pull or otherwise do aversive things with the collar; just hold it so that your dog is stuck in "boring mode."

If you patiently shape your dog to hold on to the toy, after a while they will suddenly realize that it is FUN to hold on to the toy and tug!

A Tug-N-Treat toy.

Augie immediately releases the toy and settles down when I put my hand under his chin. When I was first training this, I gave him a cookie every time he let go. Now he lets go whenever I put my hand under his chin.

Usually, that is enough to make a dog immediately drop a toy, and you can click and treat that. After a few reps you can add a cue. "That'll do" is a good release cue because it has a sing song quality and is hard to say in a nasty voice.

If your dog is a toy madman and just holding the collar is not enough to persuade him to drop it, put a piece of food under his nose and click/treat as soon as him mouth opens and the toy falls out. Depending on how obsessed your dog is with the toy, it may take many, many repetitions, but in the end you will have a reliable toy-give.

Eventually, you can fade holding the collar to just placing your hand under the dog's chin while he is still holding the toy. Your dog will understand perfectly well that there is no chance for any further play at that moment, and he will drop the toy on cue. Teaching a dog to drop a toy has the added benefit of teaching him to go from frenzied playing to calm instantly, which is an extremely important life-skill, especially for self-control-challenged dogs (which most Pigs Fly dogs are).

There are some dogs, like my Nicky, who are so toy-obsessed that they will not let go, even for a piece of food. Nicky's freaky obsession with tennis balls is legendary. He has similar obsessions with just about any toy you can name. If he finds a Frisbee, he will put his mouth on it, lick it, and hyperventilate for hours. I tried for many years to teach him a drop using all kinds of techniques and was unsuccessful. I also tried trading one toy for another, but that either had no effect on him or he wound up with both toys in his mouth. It seemed impossible to unbend his mind from his neurotic preoccupation with toys. I had resigned myself to the fact that he would never learn to give me toys. Then I hit upon a training plan that worked, and now he heels around plates of food and tennis balls off leash. Here is how you can get your ball crazy dog to do the same:

Augie is enjoying this tug game and hanging on for all he is worth. This tug game is a lot of fun for both of us.

1. Put your dog in a stay (if you have not yet trained a stay, have a friend hold your dog) and put the toy on the ground a few feet away from him.

2. Release your dog and click him as soon as he gets to the toy. This will probably stun him and chances are he will drop it. Feed him, and immediately tell him to get the toy again before he does it himself. Click as he reaches the toy.

3. If, at any point in the training session, your dog drops the toy for any reason, Click and treat that, too. Your dog will learn that he can earn treats by both getting and dropping the toy.

Why does this work so well? First of all, it is simple to teach a dog to do things, but almost impossible to teach him not to do things. With this technique you are teaching your dog an acceptable way to interact with toys, rather than trying to prevent him from interacting with them at all. Furthermore, as we discussed in Chapter Six, it is a convenient truth that, when you put a behavior on cue, the dog will tend to only do it when you ask for it. In addition, most dogs are very willing to work with you and do things your way, so long as they have the opportunity to earn the things that they want by doing what you want. If your entire training program is built around keeping your dog away from toys, your dog will spend all of his time figuring out how to get around you and get to the toys. If your training program is based on giving your dog a way to earn his toys, he will generally play by your rules.

Notwithstanding all of this talk about teaching a toy-drop, the most important rule that you must follow when playing tug games is to let your dog win often, and let him get a lot of enjoyment out of winning. I make a big show out of allowing the dog to wrest the toy from my hands, and then applaud and cheer as

See how much FUN it is to win at a tug game? Let your dog win sometimes and he will enjoy your company more than if you never let him win.

he leaps about, brandishing his prize. Much of the time I give my dog the cue to release the toy, but very often I make sure that my dog "wins." Don't worry about controlling the game by winding up with the toy, because you always have the ultimate control. If you won't play anymore, there is no game. A dog alone with a tug toy is like one hand clapping. Not much fun, at all.

It is not necessary or advisable for you to get the toy away from your dog every blessed time. If you knew someone who would only ever do something social with you if they decided it was time to do it, and then beat you every time at any game you played with them, would you want to be friends with that person? Your dog wouldn't want to be friends with them, either. Neuroscientist Jaak Panksepp has done many years of research on functions and neuropsychology of play. He makes the following observations regarding play among lab rats (New York, Affective Neuroscience, 1988):

> Play dominance clearly emerges if two rats are allowed to play together repeatedly... One rat typically tend to become the "winner," in that it ends up on top more often during pins...but the continuation of play appears to require reciprocity and the stronger partner's willingness to handicap itself. If one animal becomes a "bully" and aspires to end up on top all the time, playful activity gradually diminishes and the less successful animal begins to ignore the winner. There are reasons to believe that similar dynamics are present in human verbal play, which is a common way for folks to get to know each other and to best each other.

Nobody likes a bore. Let your dog win sometimes.

Play With Your Food
Games for the Chow Hound

Food can become a game, depending on how you dispense it. Just placing a treat in your dog's mouth is one thing, but tossing it to the side with a quick motion is more fun. Treats that are easily visible and roll and bounce as they are thrown, like cheese balls, can create excitement very quickly. If your dog does not immediately bound off after the treat, run over and pick it up yourself. Show Fido what he missed, and quickly throw it again. Repeat over and over. It will not take him long to figure out that he has to race to get the treat. This is a great game for transforming the most stoic couch potato into a lively playmate.

Another way of enticing dogs to play with food is to use toys that contain food, like the Tug-N-Treat or the stuffed bait bag we talked about in the tugging section. You can also use a treat that actually is food, like a bully stick—a foot-long piece of rolled rawhide (dried bull penis—I kid you not). Vary the presentation of your reinforcement. Let your dog smell it (but not taste it), put his mouth on it, see it, chase after you after you let him smell it, chew it while you hold it, chew it on his own for a while, chase it after you throw it. That one toy can become a dozen different reinforcements, depending on how you present it.

Even a dull scrap of bread is an exciting reinforcer if you make a game of it.

Naked Games
Graduate School

Your ultimate goal is to have a repertoire of fun things you can do with your dog to get him excited that do not require toys or food. Dog trainer Brenda Buja calls these "naked games." If your dog has a strong love for

The way you deliver a treat makes the difference between a ho-hum reinforcer and one that makes your dog vibrate with excitement. Cheese balls are OK to eat, but FANTASTIC to chase down.

naked games, you can get his attention any time, any where without the need for "props." Most naked games start out as cold, or, at best, lukewarm activities. By practice and reinforcement, they become hot activities. I call them "graduate" activities, because it takes a long time and a strong relationship for naked games to become fun for your dog. For some dogs, naked games come rather naturally, but for most dogs a substantial history of reinforcement is necessary before your dog will come to love naked games in their own right. Here are some examples of great naked games:

1. Jumping up for a hand touch.

2. Side to side hand touches.

3. Speak—just click when your dog barks, then put it on cue.

4. Jumping up on the handler.

5. Shoving dog on the chest.

6. Toe pinches—make pinching motions with your fingers as you stalk your dog and gently pinch his feet. Eventually, just the pinching motion will be enough to rev your dog up.

7. Loud smooches or backwards kisses. If your dog's size permits, lift him off of the ground while smooching.

8. Jump from side to side, keeping your body low.

9. Running around like a lunatic.

10. Clapping.

11. Spinning.

12. Play bowing.

Jumping up for a hand touch is a game that many dogs very quickly learn to love.

Training a dog to jump up on cue is an especially delightful game where dogs finally get to do the thing they naturally want to do.

Please, be sensible and safe about the naked games you play. If you are training a soft-tempered little Italian Greyhound, don't shove him around—gentle clapping while facing slightly away from him is enough. If you are training a bold Newfoundland, you can go ahead and push on him with both hands. A well socialized and friendly dog that you have raised from puppyhood may love bold games, like loud smooches, shoving, and having air blown in his face, and anyone might be perfectly safe to do those things with him. On the other hand, if you have just adopted a rescue dog and he is a little shy and you don't know much about his history, please be safe and stick to milder games, like spinning, hand touches, or play bows.

Pig Tale

One of my friends, Kathy, had a rescue Greyhound named Slicky. Because racing Greyhounds receive little or no meaningful human interaction when young, they often do not know how to enjoy being petted. Kathy would put her hand on Slicky's head, and click/treat. Poor Slicky may have been under socialized, but he was not dumb, and he quickly grew to love being patted. He so enjoyed being patted that he developed his own naked game where he would flip up Kathy's hand with his nose and earn some patting in return.

Like tug games, naked games require an "off" switch. Use the same "that'll do" phrase to signal that that the play session is over and it is time to calm down. At first your dog may jump up a few times and try to keep things going, but it is crucial that you don't give in, and don't react. Your dog will learn to understand the end-of-play-session cue very quickly, if you are consistent.

I do not advise overly rough play with any dog. Naked games are ritualized sequences that you can do with your dog to build excitement, but they are not roughhousing. You must also be careful to teach your dog how to play within bounds. Rough jumping on you, nipping, or biting are not part of naked games. If he crosses the line and becomes too rough, jumps on your and/or begins nipping, you must instantly cut off the game. No scolding is necessary or advisable—any interaction, even one that you mean to be punishing, will just be viewed as part of the game. If play escalates this way, take it as a lesson and make sure that you ramp down your next play session before it gets to that point!

I believe that mouthing is acceptable, so long as it is super-gentle mouthing. Some dogs are way too rough when they play with their mouths, but other dogs are very sweet with their mouths and seem to understand very well the fragility of human skin. If you can teach a dog to use his mouth gently in play, he has learned a lot more about who you are and how to interact with you than if you teach him not to use his mouth, ever. After all, a dog's mouth is how he connects with others. Dogs do not have opposable thumbs and they can't hold hands!

Some type/breeds of dogs are more likely to want to relate to you through their mouths than others. Northern breeds are often skillful in this way—the Alaskan Malamutes I have known all liked to use their mouth as part of their greeting/play rituals and they were always very gentle. Generally, I have found Terriers to be dismal at judging the limitations of human skin and I don't encourage them to play with their mouths. All the usual caveats apply here—if your dog is not mentally stable, or if you don't know the dog well, steer clear of playing games that involve mouths on skin.

Piggy Pointer
Just like tug games, naked games present no threat of aggression from a well-adjusted dog, and they are excellent relationship building activities. However, if your dog is fearful, reactive, or aggressive, consult a professional trainer before trying any kind of very stimulating play, especially play that involves teeth.

The beauty of naked games is that, in every single one of them, you are the main reinforcer. Your dog is looking forward to the possibility of playing with you. You don't need to be holding food, toys or props—you have actually become reinforcing for your dog. Simply being near you becomes very exciting for your dog and, once you have that, the rest is easy.

8

Training With SAFETY

How to Teach Your Dog Any Behavior

In the next chapter, you are going to learn how to teach some basic behaviors that every dog—especially Pigs Fly dogs—should learn in order to get along in society. Before we do that, I want you to get acquainted with the steps that you will take to teach them. Every behavior will be taught the same way, using the Pigs Fly system. You will shape and strengthen the behaviors you want using your new knowledge of how to use reinforcers. We are going to teach each behavior with **SAFETY:**

Shape it

Add a cue

Frequent but short sessions

Energize your dog's behaviors with hot reinforcers

Take it on the road very gradually

Yield on your requirements when you change something

Let's review the steps we will take to teach each behavior.

Shape it. Shape the behavior as you learned in Chapter Four. Begin in a neutral environment, like your kitchen or living room, whenever possible without resorting to luring or prompting. Use small approximations as you learned to do in your free shaping sessions. To review:

1. Break the behavior down into small approximations.

2. Reinforce the first approximation until your dog is offering it again and again.

3. Once your dog clearly offers the first approximation and you have reinforced it several times, stop clicking it.

4. Watch carefully for the "improvement" that your dog will offer on that behavior, and click that. Many dogs will get a little frenzied at this stage and start throwing out all kinds of behaviors. Stay alert and be ready to click the behavior you are looking for when it comes along!

If your dog does not offer improvements, or walks away and stops working, you probably tried to raise the bar too quickly. For shaping to work, each approximation needs to be solid in your dog's mind before you move on to the next step. Sometimes you may only need to reinforce an approximation two times for your dog to "have it," and sometimes you may need to reinforce it dozens of times. It depends on the dog and the behavior your are trying to teach.

Add a cue. When you would bet $100 that your dog is about to do the behavior you have just shaped, add a cue. At first you add the cue as the dog is doing the behavior, not before. Why is that? It seems more efficient to add the cue before you get the behavior, but it is not. Let's say you are trying to teach your dog to sit by luring your hand over their head with food. It is natural and realistic to expect that your dog will not get it "right" the first few times. You raise your hand over your dogs head and say "sit" and your dog does nothing. The next time you raise your hand and say "sit" he takes a step sideways. You raise your hand over your dog's head again, you say "sit" again and he jumps up at your hand. What does "sit" mean to your dog, now? Let's see. Your dog has paired the word "sit" with: 1) no response; 2) stepping sideways; and 3) jumping up at your hand. If he ascribes any meaning to the word "sit" at all, it will be one of those three behaviors. Even if you succeed on the fourth try and actually get him to sit, the command "sit" is a now a multiple choice question. It will take many, many correct repetitions to counteract the "incorrect" responses. On the other hand, if you waited until you were sure that your dog was already in the process of sitting, and then added the cue, "sit" would only ever mean "sit," and it would take far fewer repetitions to get the behavior on cue. That is much easier for everyone involved. Gradually, you can start saying "sit" before your dog sits, and a cue is born.

It usually does not make any difference what word you use to cue any particular behavior. What is important is that you say whatever cue you use in the same exact way each time. Dogs do not speak English. Even when we manage to form an association in their minds between a spoken word and a behavior or consequence, they still don't speak English. They are responding to a particular sound, not a particular word. When you are coming up with your cues for behaviors, think of them as a musical notes that you will want to consistently sing the same way each time.

Frequent but short sessions. Your sessions should always be very short—no more than a few minutes at a time, and as frequent as is practical. Contrary to what you might think, lengthy formal training sessions are not generally advisable for a Pigs Fly dog. Studies have been done that show that more learning takes place in several short sessions than one long session, even where the long session is considerably longer than the sum of the short sessions. Thus, your dog will learn more quickly if you give him three, five minute sessions spread out during the course of the day (fifteen minutes, total), than if you set aside an entire hour for training.

When you are first teaching a behavior, you could even break down the sessions into a matter of seconds. Teaching loose leash walking? Reward the dog for anywhere from one step to 10 seconds of walking politely on leash 20 times a day and he will learn more quickly than if you trained heeling for a solid hour daily. This is especially true of Pigs Fly dogs. Biddable dogs can do long sessions of heeling or any other kind of training, because they were bred to spend long days in the field, taking direction from their handlers. Is a long session the best way to teach any dog, Pigs Fly or not? Probably not, but because the majority of performance dogs are biddable breeds and can endure long sessions, training has traditionally taken place in larger chunks and included a lot more per session than a Pigs Fly dog can take.

Short training sessions also make it easier for the trainer to be very precise and accurate. Most people cannot pay full attention to training their dog for an hour. The result is that some rewardable behaviors will go unreinforced, and many timing mistakes will be made, thereby reinforcing the wrong behavior. This will pollute the properly reinforced behaviors and stretch out the time it will take to teach them. If, on the other hand, you set out with a clear picture in your mind of what you want to reinforce and only have to hold that picture for a matter of minutes or seconds, you are much more likely to be accurate in shaping the behavior you want. It is part of the agreement you make with your dog every time you train him—give me the behavior that I am looking for and I promise to reinforce it 100% of the time. The closer you come to that 100%, the faster your dog will learn, and the stronger the behaviors will be in the face of distractions.

Piggy Pointer

When I say that you need to reinforce a behavior 100% of the time, that does not mean that you have to reinforce, for instance, every single step of heeling or loose leash walking. Based on where you and your dog are in your training, you will have decided in advance how many repetitions of the behavior the dog needs to give you before reinforcing—one step, five steps, or twenty steps. You might just be looking for a particularly well executed behavior—a really fast sit or down, for instance. The point is that, in a short session, you will be able to maintain a clear picture in your mind of what you are looking for and you will be focused enough to remember to reinforce when you get that picture from your dog.

Energize your dog's behavior with hot reinforcers. Once you have the behavior and it is on cue, and your dog is performing correctly almost every single time at home in a neutral environment, you mix in hot reinforcers to create excitement about the behavior. Remember the slot machine and make yourself as unpredictable as possible. Here are some example of hot reinforcers and how I use them for specific dogs:

1. The Bull Terrier likes balls. It's very easy to dispense this reinforcer because you can carry a ball with you in your pocket or bait pouch.

Use the reinforcers that your dog naturally likes. This Rhodesian Ridgeback might not care much for a game of tug, but playing with a lure is very enjoyable for him.

2. The Rhodesian Ridgeback likes lure coursing. Although you can't carry a lure course in your pocket, you could carry some kind of lure on a string and run away like mad, dragging it behind you. Or maybe you are lucky and rich and you do have a lure course set up in your back yard with an assistant ready to start pulling the lure—you could release him to go chase it.

3. The Norwich Terrier likes to hunt down vermin. Even if you could carry a chipmunk in your pocket and present it to your terrier as a reinforcer, it would not be a very nice thing to do. You could get a furry toy on a string and drag it along the ground quickly in a convincing imitation of some small prey animal. By all means do not shove the toy in the dog's face—pull it and shake it along the ground in an erratic pattern that mimics a small rodent running away from the dog. I do know some people who cut the tails off of road kill squirrels and use them as bait. I think

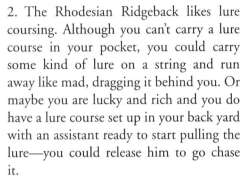

This Norwich Terrier goes crazy for a furry mouse toy on a string!

I would have a hard time with this one on multiple grounds, (including and especially the possibility of disease or fleas), but I take it on faith that dead-squirrel-tails make great motivators.

4. The Pharaoh Hound likes to sniff. Good thing you read the previous section and put this one on cue! If the dog does what you want, he gets released to sniff. Be creative—scope out the area you will be training in before hand and see if there are any animal burrows around. You could run over to the burrow after releasing your dog and give him something really good to sniff.

5. Here are some other ideas. A dog that is "birdy" might like a toy that flutters like a bird. Another dog might really like to dig—bring a little spade in your pocket and start a hole with him. I used to bring a garden trowel to training class so I could dig a hole for one of my Bull Terriers and she loved it! I had a dog in class that really went crazy for used tissues. Yes, I let him have pieces of tissue. Some dogs love soap bubbles, or having you tear up pieces of grass and toss them in the air. If any kind of prey drive activity was high on your dog's list, save up your old 16 oz water bottles, put a couple of tablespoons of un-popped popcorn in them, and put them in an old sock. If you feel like sewing you can make a fur sleeve with a handle and sew Velcro on the top so you can change the bottles as they become crushed. The crunching, rattling, action of this toy is a big hit in certain circles.

Take it on the road very gradually. Once your dog is performing a behavior flawlessly in your kitchen, move into the living room. Once he can perform in every room of your house, try the back porch, then the back yard, then the front porch, then the sidewalk in front of your house. Gradually work up to the point where your dog will do behaviors anywhere, anytime.

The mistake that most people make is they assume they have a right to go anywhere with their dog at anytime. This is not true. You have to train your dog before you can go for walks, and then train some more before

The way you use a toy can make all the difference. This bird dog might not care much for a toy dragged on the ground, but he goes crazy for a ribbon on a stick that flutters like a bird.

you go for walks in very stimulating places, like a trail or at a crowded park. It does not take much, but you have to put in the time to gradually raise the stimulation level of the environment in which you expect your dog to perform. Remember, every time that you change the context, your beautiful behaviors that you trained at home might fall apart. You may have a great loose lead walk on Main Street, but as soon as you go to New Street, your dog is a mess. Don't despair—the behaviors are still there, but you need to go back to the last place where your dog was good, and gradually work your way up again

Pig-tionary
Context: the circumstances and conditions in which a dog is performing his behaviors. Physical location is the most obvious context, but anything that changes, different people, different smells, different position of handler, are all changes in context and will impact the way your dog performs.

You may also find that, when you try to take your dog out in public and work the behaviors he has learned, he suddenly has no interest in his hot reinforcers. It is very common for a dog to refuse his favorite toys or games when in a public situation. A dog has to be comfortable to play, and if he is stressed by his surroundings, he may be too inhibited or distracted to enjoy his usual games. Keep working on behaviors your dog will perform, using whatever reinforcers he will take, and don't worry about it if he has no interest in his beloved squeaky toy. So long as you are using your hot reinforcers at home, a good association is being made between the behavior and the reinforcer and the behavior is being strengthened.

Yield on your requirements when you change something. At home, you may be able to give your dog one dry dog biscuit in exchange for a sit, a down, a paw wave, plus a spin, and he might perform beautifully for you. Don't expect him to be that way when you take him out on the trail. You may have to drop your expectations back and reinforce him for any kind of attention at all, never mind asking him to perform any behaviors or tricks. In this example, you have changed location, moving from a familiar, neutral environment to a more stimulating one, and you have to set the bar lower for your dog. Even something as simple as having a visitor over to your house is a change for you dog. Asking your dog to do something on your right side instead of your left side is a big change. If you have shaped your dog to sit right next to you on your left side by gradually shaping him to sit closer and closer to you, don't expect a close sit on your right side immediately. Reinforce any sit at all on the right side, at first, and then shape your way to a close sit.

Now that you have the blueprint, let's move on to building behaviors!

9

The Foundation of Everything

Basic Behaviors

In this chapter, you will learn how to use the SAFETY method to teach eight "foundation behaviors." If you can call upon your dog to do these eight behaviors, you will prepared for and able to handle most any situation or problem you might encounter. Think of them as "Reading, 'Riting, and 'Rithmetic" for your dog.

Take a Load Off Your Feet
Sit/Down

Sits and downs are behaviors that all well-mannered dogs should be able to do without fail. Easy to say, but not so easy for Pigs Fly dogs, of course. However, using what you have learned so far, teaching sits and downs is a piece of cake!

Sit is a simple behavior to learn, unless you have a Pigs Fly dog.

Sit

Shape. You can shape a sit by clicking for just a little leg bend and approximating bigger and bigger leg bends until your dog actually sits. Alternatively, if you are a patient person, you can carry your clicker around with you for waiting your dog to sit and then click that. Either way (or a combination of both) will work fine. Try to reward your dog while he is still in the sit position, if possible. It will help reinforce to your dog that sitting pays off. If your dog gets up after you click and you cannot feed him in position, go ahead and feed him anyway—don't sweat it and don't say anything to him. The click signifies that he has performed the behavior, and he is free to do anything he wants after that—he is within bounds to get up. Just see if you can sneak the food in a little faster next time so he remains sitting while you feed.

Piggy Pointer
Don't be discouraged if at first you find it hard to catch your dog in the act of sitting and click him in time. Even though you have a clicker around your neck or on your wrist, you still might get flustered and miss clicking the behavior. You might pick up a butter knife instead of the clicker, try to click the butter knife, remember your clicker, push the wrong end, and only succeed in clicking when your dog has gotten up and is walking away. It takes a little practice to be quick enough to catch behaviors, but it is so easy once you get it. Keep trying! The worst thing that will happen is that you miss clicking the behavior you want, and that is no big deal. You will get it, eventually.

Keep your hand low and feed from at or below the dog's nose level in order to help keep her seated.

Add a cue. Once your dog is merrily running up to you and offering a sit, you can start to add the word "sit." Be sure, at first, to add your cue when his butt is actually on the ground (we don't want him to think "sit" means "crouch!". Gradually add the cue earlier and earlier. A new behavior is born.

Frequent but short sessions. "Sit" is an easy one to incorporate into your daily life. After an initial session or two, excite your dog by giving him unscheduled "pop quizzes" throughout the day. Ask for just one sit, click and treat it, and go back to doing what you were doing. Not only will this teach your dog to sit very quickly, it will also teach him that he never knows when he might be called upon to do something fun that can earn him a great reward, so he had better be paying attention!

Energize your dog's behavior with hot reinforcers. When adding your hot reinforcers, be sure that you have clicked the sit before you produce the hot reinforcer. Click, wait a beat, and dispense your hot reinforcer. The reason you have to do this is that you may inadvertently click as your dog is jumping up to play with you. What do you think the problem with that is? Well, keep in mind that you will get whatever you click. If you click as your dog is jumping up in the air to get a toy, then the behavior you have built is "sit, then jump up in the air." It is common to see dogs who pop up right after a sit, and this is usually why.

Take it on the road gradually. Follow all the rules of slowly building your dog's ability to sit anywhere. Just like you did at home, give him pop quizzes randomly when you are out and about. Sit is one of the most important foundation behaviors you can build—it is hard for your dog to get into trouble if he is sitting, so we want him to be able to do it any time, any where, without fail.

It takes a lot of practice to get your dog to the point where he will sit anywhere, anytime, no matter what distractions are around him.

Yield on your requirements when you change something. Remember that just because your dog sits in front of you in your kitchen, does not mean he will sit next to you at the pet store. You may almost have to re-teach the sit when you change the context, but it usually will not take long to do this. The "sit" behavior is in there and you just have to bring it out again.

Down

Shape. You can free shape a down by clicking just a slight head dip, and then a bigger head dip, then shoulders leaning down, and so forth, until you have a down. As always, this is my preferred method to teach the behavior, but I have to admit that it takes some skill to shape a down for many Pigs Fly dogs. This is one of those places where it is good training economy to introduce a lure. Get down on the floor (your exact position will depend on how limber you are) and make a little bridge by bending one of your knees. Lure your dog under your leg and, as he ducks his head down, click that. You can approximate the down just the same way as if you were free shaping it, but you are getting the dog started by luring him into a position where he is likely to start offering the behavior. If your dog is huge and you are small or if you are not too flexible, sit in a chair or on a low stool and prop your leg up on a milk crate.

When using a lure to teach the down, you might be tempted to click only when your dog actually lies down, rather than clicking each approximation. Your dog would certainly learn to lie down that way, but, as we discussed earlier in this chapter, the behavior will be stronger and more durable if you click and treat each approximation.

If you click for a lowered head, the elbows will almost certainly begin to bend soon after. As you can see in the third picture, there is the tiniest bit of bend in the elbow—reinforce that heavily. Once the elbows hit the ground, the rear end will plop down soon after.

Add a cue. The cue you use will depend on how you taught the down. If you free shaped it, you add a verbal cue—I use "down." If you lured the down, it is easy to use a similar hand motion to the lure to cue the down. You can start fading the food by hiding it in the palm of your hand as you lure the down. Once your dog is responding to the hand motion reliably without actually seeing the food, try it without the food hidden in the palm of your hand. You should be able to fool him once—as long as you click and treat quickly from the other hand, he will be willing to lie down again without the piece of food to lure him down.

Frequent but short sessions. Like, sit, down is easy to work on throughout the day. After an initial training session or two, you can give your dog a "pop quiz" throughout the day on "down."

Energize your dog's behavior with hot reinforcers. The hotter the reinforcer, the better. If your dog gets pinwheel eyes over a ball or anything else, nothing is more useful than teaching him to assume the down position before getting his treasured object. Not only will he learn to love lying down, he will learn an important lesson about self control—he has to do a calm behavior in order to earn an exciting one. Just as with the sit, be certain that your dog is lying down and you have clicked it before you offer the hot reinforcer.

Take it on the road very gradually. There are some special considerations about "down" that you should keep in mind when planning how to take it on the road. Many dogs are reluctant to lie down in a strange place. This is natural and, from an evolutionary standpoint, probably a good strategy; a wild dog that casually lies down anywhere without checking out the area thoroughly first is putting himself at risk for all kinds of potential harm. One of the first warning signals for me that my dogs are stressed is when they don't lie down or sit when asked. Lying down is a vulnerable position, and a dog has to feel comfortable and safe to want to do it. Or, (sigh, yes, here it comes), you have to own a breed of dog that has "down" as a default behavior. That would be most of the herding group. Herding dogs have to lie down in an instant on the shepherd's command. That is the way the shepherd controls the dog that is moving the flock. You will notice that many herding dogs flop themselves down frequently of their own accord. On the contrary, "down" is not in a terrier's vocabulary—what does "down" have to do with killing badgers? Again, it appears that more "working in cooperation" type dogs have been bred to be willing to "assume the position," even in circumstances where it is not natural for a dog to do so.

Then be sensible and don't ask for a down if your dog is obviously very excited and unlikely to respond properly. Wait until he has his brain engaged and is paying attention to you before you ask for a down.

Yield on your requirements when you change something. If your dog lies down like a pro at home, but he suddenly won't lie somewhere new, here are some troubleshooting tips. Give him a little more time to check out his surroundings and feel comfortable. That may or may not be all you have to do, depending on where your dog is in his training divided by how overwhelming the place is. Go back to behaviors he will do under the circumstances and repeat them lots of times. Maybe a nice, centering, hand touch (which you will learn how to teach in this chapter), maybe a fun trick that he likes, such as shake, maybe some loose leash walking with attention. Go as far down the behavior hierarchy as you have to. If all that your dog can do is stand there and look at you, click that attention. These "solid ground" behaviors will help settle your dog and get his brain working again. Once he is back in a thinking mode, you will most likely find that he will sit and down easily in the new place.

If you have a very large dog, it might be helpful to sit on a stool when luring her into a down. Click and treat as soon as her elbows begin to bend. Then give a big jackpot here to reinforce that idea that "down" is a great position to be in.

Something for Nothing
Stay

"Stay" is the ultimate management tool and an indispensable behavior. Your life will be inconvenient if your dog does not have a stay. You will find yourself constantly shoving, jostling, and diving to get things before your dog latches on to them. If your dog is possessive about toys or food, or has any other resource guarding issues, you need to be able to control any situation by putting him in a stay. Going through a door with a dog

Stay—the indispensable behavior.

that does not have a stay is a chore; you find yourself either body slamming with him as you both try to squeeze through at the same time, or physically shoving him back as you attempt to get through the door unmolested. A good stay makes your life a lot easier and saves a lot of unpleasantness in the long run.

Holding still in one place is a very abstract concept for Pigs Fly dogs. Biddable dogs, on the other hand, tend to be hanging on their master's next command. Remember the Sheltie in Scott and Fuller's study who "gave the subjective impression of standing around and waiting for someone to tell them what to do"? That dog might settle in just fine with the idea of doing nothing until told otherwise. Your dog, on the other hand, is a Dog Of Action, and the world beckons him. Sniff, dig, chew, hunt, run are all very plausible activities for your dog—stay is not.

Shape

1. Let's begin with making your dog understand what stay means. Stand in front of your dog. Just wait until your dog is motionless and click/treat that. The position your dog is in is not relevant, but you might find it easier if you ask your dog to sit first because it takes a little more effort to move from a sit than it does from, for instance, a stand.

2. Reward the sit, and then wait a fraction of a second and click/treat again. Whatever position your dog is in, make sure that you deliver the treat in such a way that your dog does not have to move to get it.

3. Continue click/treating almost continuously until your dog breaks position then stop, go about your business for a while, and come back and set up to try again. You want to pause long enough so that your dog understands that his opportunity for reinforcement ended when he broke position. Please do not say anything at all to your dog when he breaks position. We don't want feedback from you to become a part of this behavior. This is about letting him figure things out for himself. He will see soon enough what gets him an opportunity for treats and what does not.

4. After a few reps of click/treating for remaining motionless, you will see the glimmer of recognition flash in his eyes—he will think about breaking position, and then catch himself and remain seated. Jackpot the heck out of that one. Soon you will see your dog almost squinting with the effort of staying as he sits there—you can just see the bubble over his head that says, "Look, look, I'm st-aaaaying!" Once you get this kind of recognition, you can move on to the next step.

5. Next, build in a little hesitation before you click. You should still be standing right in front of your dog. Hesitate just one second before clicking. Once your dog has that down pat, you can hesitate two seconds sometimes, one second sometimes, and a split second other times. Ping pong your way up until you are doing variations on five seconds.

6. If you can get your dog to stay for five seconds in your living room with you standing right in front of him—congratulations, you have done a great job! Now you can systematically build up the length of your dog's stays. Still standing right in front of your dog, you will build up to a one minute stay over a few sessions. Once you get to this stage, you should not use the clicker. Just walk back and reward him for staying. Why not use a clicker in this instance? "Click ends the behavior" is a maxim of dog training. What that means is that, once you click a behavior, your dog is free to break position and do whatever he wants. For that reason, use a clicker in the very early stages of teaching a stay to isolate the "holding still" behavior, but move to just reinforcing without clicking the instant you feel the dog understands that not moving earns him a reward. Once you are building up to several second stays, it is counterproductive to click, have your dog get up (which is perfectly correct), and then have to ask him to sit again—that is really teaching a bunch of short stays rather than one long one.

Use the reinforcement schedules in the Resources section for your training plan. Go slowly and don't be in a hurry to get long stays. You know you are doing the right thing if your dog is not breaking position as you gradually raise the amount of time you ask him to stay. If your dog is breaking position, you are asking for too much.

Be very specific about what you are shaping. You want to select and reinforce a complete absence of motion. If you reinforce your dog, even though you left him in a down and he started doing the commando crawl towards you, the behavior of "stay" is going to be murky in his mind. If the commando crawl is OK, how about crouching? How about getting up? Stay means stay, and you should not reinforce any movement, even if it is in the same family as the original position. If your dog starts to crawl towards you, go back to him calmly and, without any comment, move him away from the spot where you had him in a stay. Then go back and re-set him up. If your dog is breaking position a lot, drop back to a length of time where he does not break position. However short an interval is needed to be certain that he will stay in position, go down to that level. Don't be discouraged, you can build back up to a longer stay, but you have to get the behavior first. Again, please do not tell him he is wrong if he changes position—things will go much faster in the long run if you just don't reinforce him and make him figure out why he is not getting his cookie.

Piggy Pointer
The only changes in position you should accept in a stay are "settling in" changes in position. For instance, if your dog lies down in a "Sphinx" position, with his back legs tucked directly underneath him, and after a little while he rolls over on his hip and stretches his back legs out, or lies down completely flat on his side, that is great. It means he is relaxing and committed to staying in position.

The bottom line is that it is better to have your dog remain completely immobile for five seconds than have him slowly crawl towards you over three minutes and wind up four feet from where he started. That is not a "stay," that is a "slow crawl towards you."

Add a cue. Once your dog is offering to stay in position for ten seconds, you can add a cue. I use a verbal "stay." Although you have built up to your dog offering a ten second stay, when you first add the cue you should reinforce your dog immediately for remaining in position. You can build back up quickly to a ten second stay, with a cue "stay" at the beginning.

Frequent but short sessions. Whatever level of stay you are working on, practicing once a day is very helpful. Stay is a behavior that often gets neglected because it is kind of boring for the trainer. Put in regular effort for a minute or two each day, and you will be richly rewarded. Don't be discouraged if it seems like your dog will never learn to stay, or if you thought he knew how to stay and then he seemed to forget. The first time I tried to teach a dog to stay I was sure I was doing something wrong, because it took so infernally long for him to get it. People sometimes assume that their training technique is wrong because their dog is not getting a particular behavior. Nine times out of ten, the trainer is doing the right thing, but it takes lots of repetitions in every conceivable situation over a period of time for a dog to truly "get" a behavior. Pigs Fly dogs may need more repetitions than other breeds—be patient!

Energize your dog's behavior with hot reinforcers. When you are adding toys and games and other hot reinforcers, be careful that you do not always release your dog forward to the toy/game. Sometimes throw the toy/start the game behind him, sometimes to one side or the other, sometimes give him the toy/start the game right there before he breaks position. If your dog always is breaking forward out of his stay, he will begin to anticipate that and he might break before you want him to. As always, be unpredictable and your dog will wait to see what you will do next instead of taking matters into his own hands.

People who own biddable dogs often do not have to go through the step of pairing hot reinforcers with stays because the hot reinforcer is right there—their handler! If you have a Beagle, on the other hand, and you put him in a stay and walk away, his first thought is, "Cool! I can go sniff things now, and she can't stop me!" Remember, by pairing "stay" with the opportunity to go sniff, "stay" becomes a very exciting activity. If you are fair with your dog and give him an opportunity to access his favorite foods, toys and activities in exchange for holding a stay, he will be much less likely to break his stay and avail himself of all the goodies within his reach. Even a Pigs Fly dog has some semblance of working in cooperation with you—if he feels his interests are represented fairly in your training program, he will show some self-control and do it your way.

Take it on the road very gradually. Learning to stay in the face of incredible distraction is an important self-control lesson for dogs. Follow the rules of gradually introducing the stay in more and more stimulating locations. Be especially careful not to ask for a stay if your dog is so excited that there is no way he is going to succeed in staying.

Yield on your requirements when you change something. You are on your way to building one of the most important behaviors in your dog's repertoire. A dog that can stay still for ten seconds in your living room probably understands the concept of stay. Expanding that concept to encompass staying in place for five minutes with you standing twenty feet away with distractions all around is a different task. The elements of a stay are:

Distance

Distraction

Duration

You will have to introduce each of these elements separately, and yield on the others until the new element is learned. Right now, your distance from your dog is approximately two feet, you are working in an area that has no distractions, and the duration that your dog can hold his stay is ten seconds.

Distance. We are going to add distance between you and your dog, so we will relax our requirements on duration and distraction.

1. Although you have worked your dog up to the point where he will hold his stay with distractions, you need to go back to the least distracting place you can think. Start again in your kitchen or the most boring place you can think of for your dog. We want to take away any distractions he might find in a more exciting place.

2. Ask your dog to "stay."

3. Move one foot back and forth and click if your dog does not move. Don't try for any duration of stay. You just want your dog to understand that stay means "stay in place, even if your handler is moving around." Do that a few times until it looks like your dog understands that he has to stay in position while you move in order to earn his cookie.

4. Next, take one step away from your dog and step right back again. Click and feed him if he does not move. Work your way up to being able to take two steps away and return immediately. Click when you get back to your dog if he did not move.

5. Once you can take one step away from your dog and he did not move, you no longer should use the clicker to mark the behavior for the same reasons that were discussed in the section of shaping the stay. Now you can start working your way up to being able to walk however far from your dog you would like—I suggest twenty feet as a nice goal.

Distraction. Are you able to walk ten or twenty feet away from your dog while he stays in place? Bravo! A stay is a great achievement and you should have a big sense of accomplishment if you have gotten to this point. The next step towards a perfect stay is to add distractions in a controlled environment. It is important that you introduce distractions systematically because distractions are so much more… well, distracting for a Pigs Fly dog than for biddable dogs. Biddable dogs have it clear that they need to keep focused on their handlers, and the distractions are just interference with the task at hand. Pigs Fly dogs think that the distractions are the task at hand. Fortunately for us Pigs Fly owners, working with distractions is really a fun game. There is only one rule: anything distracting means "stay in place and maintain eye contact with your handler."

To train this, begin in your kitchen again, and go back to standing right in front of your dog—relax on the distance requirement. Get a friend or family member to act as a distractor. Have them walk 10, 20 or even 30 feet away from your dog. Start the distractor as far away as necessary for your dog to remain in position and keep his eyes on you. As soon as the distractor comes into your dog's field of vision, immediately click and treat for maintaining eye contact. Even if your dog can hold his stay for ten seconds, click immediately. You are relaxing the duration requirement while you work on distraction. Your dog may swivel his head to look, but click him anyway if he looks back at you right away.

Gradually work your way up to someone walking right in front of your dog, right behind your dog, even stepping over your dog. Here is a sample progression of how you would train your dog to stay with distractions:

1. Have someone put their hand out as if to touch your dog.

2. Have someone touch your dog's head.

3. Have someone pat your dog.

4. Have someone crumple paper near your dog.

5. Have someone move his arms in front of and around your dog.

6. Have someone do jumping jacks.

Or whatever other crazy thing you can think of, and click and treat your dog every time for remaining in position and maintaining eye contact.

Soon your dog will get really happy and excited when the "distracter" comes around, because he will know that means he is about to get an opportunity to earn cookies. The important concept that your dog learns is that he has a behavior to fall back on when his environment gets crazy or stressful. The crazy stuff that might otherwise make him react in a wild fashion instead becomes a cue to calmly look at his handler. That is something any dog can understand and it is a pleasure to live with a dog that has been trained this way.

You set up distractions this way in a controlled environment so you can make sure your dog is set up for successes. Once your dog learns the general concept, this lesson will (with practice) carry over when you take your dog out on the road and ask him to stay in a crowded park. He will eventually view all the hub-bub as a cue to keep his eyes on you and his butt in place.

Duration. Once your dog has the basic idea of the stay behavior, you can gradually start building up to having your dog stay for longer and longer periods of time. The best way to do this is to ask your dog for an average number of seconds of stay and gradually increase that average. For instance, you might start with asking for an average of three seconds of stay, which means you would ask for one, then four, then five, then two seconds of stay. Three is about the average you are asking for. Then you can increase to an average of, say, five seconds. You might reinforce five, then four, then one second then ten seconds—the average is about five seconds. You can build up a long and very reliable stay by using this method of reinforcement. The important thing is that you build up your average (mean) duration by "bouncing" around it. That way your dog never figures out that it is getting harder and harder the way he would if you just did two seconds today, three seconds tomorrow, four seconds the next day, etc. The randomness of the reinforcement also maintains excitement because your dog never knows when he might be in for a treat.

Morgan Spector has graciously allowed me to reprint the reinforcement schedules from his book, *Clicker Training For Obedience*. They can be found in the Resouces section at the end of the book. Use them as a guideline for teaching stays or any other behavior that requires duration or repetitions of behaviors.

Let's say that your dog will stay for a minute (duration), will stay if you walk twenty feet away (distance), and will stay if someone is hitting him in the head with a peanut butter and jelly sandwich (distraction), but just not all at the same time. Now you should start combining these elements:

1. Walk out 20 feet from your dog and then see how much duration you can build. Start at one, then two seconds, and build up to one minute using the same schedule of reinforcement you used for teaching the one minute stay with you standing right in front of your dog.

2. You can start standing a little further and further from you dog as the distractors do their thing until you are 20 feet away.

3. You can start practicing all of these things in other, gradually more exciting, places.

If you want a longer stay, a stay further away from you, a stay with you in another room, or a stay in the middle of the county fair, you can work your way up to it using the guidelines in this section.

I Can't Take My Eyes Off of You!
Attention Walking

This is what attention walking looks like. Ruby gladly offers attention because she has been reinforced heavily over the years for looking at me and walking by my side.

Walking politely on leash is another behavior that many dogs do quite easily, but it can be a formidable task with a Pigs Fly dog. It seems like Pigs Fly dogs are always either pulling your arm out of the socket or planting themselves into the ground and refusing to move. One of the top reasons people bring their dog to professional trainers is that they want to be able to take a walk and return home with their arms the same length as when they set out, and not need extensive chiropractic attention to return their shoulders to good repair. There are also lots of people out there who would love to take a nice, long, bonding walk with their beloved pet, but Fido just plain will not budge. The answer to both problems is exactly the same. We are going to teach your dog that walking close to you is a very rewarding experience that he can look forward to.

What you are going to teach your dog is what I call "attention walking." You will teach your dog to walk right next to you on your left side and keep his eyes glued to you. This will be the foundation behavior for loose leash walking. You may not want or need your dog to be in this exact position with full eye contact all the time, but it is essential that you have it to draw upon. There are lots of times when it is handy to have a dog that walks right next to you with attention: when you are in a crowd; when there are other not-so-nice dogs around; when you don't want your dog walking all over the place and getting wrapped around a telephone pole; or when you just want to get past some big distraction. In these situations you need to be able to get your dog into attention walking mode and get past the problem. Attention walking, when reinforced, is also a fun game for dogs to play and they love being asked to do it. If your dog is fearful or reluctant, attention walking makes him feel safe. His world is narrowed down to you and him, and timid dogs find that very comforting.

You will also teach another, more casual, walk, but you need the foundation of the attention walk, first. Trust me, it will be much easier to get casual walking without pulling if you teach attention walking first.

Shape. If you have worked on free shaping attention, teaching attention walking is a snap because it is really just a moving version of the attention behavior. Ideally, you will teach this behavior without a leash. Begin in a safely enclosed, boring environment. If you don't have a fenced-in area, go to an open area and put your dog on a 30 foot long line.

1. Free shape some attention (as in Chapter Five). Click and treat a few times just to get your dog's motor running.

2. Start meandering around while keeping an eye your dog. Don't say anything to him—let him become curious about what you are doing so he will come over to investigate. Imagine an area that extends about three feet directly off of your left side, and extends to about two feet in front of you. We call this the "magic circle" because, anytime your dog puts any part of his body in this area, he is magically going to make the clicker go off and he will get a treat. You are going to reinforce your dog for staying in this area again and again until it becomes like sacred ground to which he will always gravitate.

I am going to click the dog here. Ultimately, I would like her to be closer to me, but this is a good start.

After I click, I deliver the treat so that the dog is in the position in which I would ultimately like her to be.

3. After you click your dog for entering the magic circle, deliver the treat close to the outside of your left knee to reinforce closeness to you. Eventually, you will want your dog to be right next to you, and feeding close to you is a way to get him to anticipate that he should stay close. Don't be discouraged if you have trouble feeding your dog in position. Feeding so your dog is in position is another skill and you will get better at it with practice. It will help you a lot if you carry a piece of food in your left hand so you are ready to feed in position. Try to think in advance exactly how you will deliver a treat to help your dog maintain position, and keep trying.

4. At some point, you will probably notice that your dog is thinking hard, and then scurrying in next to you. A dog at this stage looks like a kid, waiting for just the right moment and then hopping into a double Dutch jump rope. That's when you know that he understands he has to step in the magic circle. Once you see the light bulb go on in this way, and your dog is offering the behavior of stepping into the magic circle, reinforce it a few more times, and then up the ante. Ask for him to look at you while he works. Chances are, he has been looking at you pretty intensely since the session began, but let's pick it out and reinforce it, just to be sure. Now you will only click if your dog steps into the circle and is looking at you. Reinforce that many times until your dog is obviously offering to keep his eyes on you.

5. Next, shape him to be close to you. If you can get your dog to take a step or two in the magic circle and keep his eyes on you, you should be very proud of yourself. Your dog is well on the way to understanding that you want him to walk by your side and pay attention to you. Gradually make the magic circle smaller and smaller so he has to come in closer and closer to you to earn his click. How many sessions it will take until your dog is taking a step or two right next to you on your left side while maintaining eye contact depends on the dog and your skill. Some dogs can be shaped to a perfect attention walking position by a skillful trainer in one session, and some will need weeks of work.

Pig Tale
I can usually teach a dog to attention walk in one or two sessions, but not every dog is that easy. My dog Ursa took literally months before she would put together walking, being close to my side, and looking at me. She did get it eventually, though, and now she loves to bounce along and look up eagerly at me. However long it takes, that is the right amount of time for you and your dog. Don't get discouraged and keep trying!

Take the physical make up of your dog into account when deciding how to set up this behavior. A short, stubby dog, like a Pug, a Bassett Hound, or a Bulldog, will find it difficult to be both right by your side and crane his head up to look at you. You might even cause injury to his neck by asking him to move in that position for a long time. If you have a stocky dog like this, give up either closeness or eye contact so your dog can be comfortable and healthy. Many people shape their stubby or short dogs to look at their handler's leg as they walk. Whatever you choose is fine, as long as you have a clearly defined idea of what you want and you try to shape your dog to that ideal position as closely as possible.

6. Now you can start building up the number of steps your dog will take. Is your little friend right next to you, taking a step or two with his eyes glued to you? If you answered "Yes," you have done a great job, and, you are ready to start putting together longer and longer stretches of attention walking.

7. Be careful to be random about how many steps of walking in position you reward, and work up to long stretches of walking very slowly. Don't always ask for more steps—sometimes reinforce two steps, sometimes four, sometimes six, and then two again. You want to keep your dog guessing! Use the guidelines under the Duration heading in the section on teaching the stay. Because it is hard to keep all of this in mind and come up with an appropriate reinforcement schedule on the spot, you will find suggested schedules for reinforcement in the Resources section. You can use them as a daily plan for building loose leash walking.

Add a cue. Once your dog is walking for a few steps in just the position you like, you can add a cue. I use the phrase "let's go" to signal my dogs that I want them to walk next to me in this way. When you are adding a cue, be careful exactly when you add it. For example, you want to make sure that you first add your cue when your dog is moving in position. Be careful that you don't add the cue when your dog is slowing down, looking away or stopping to get a treat. Once the association between the cue and the correct behavior is made, you can start earlier and earlier until it actually prompts your dog to start walking with you.

Frequent but short sessions. Although you may only actually take your dog on a walk once a day or every few days or weeks, you can practice attention walking anytime throughout the day, in your yard or in your living room. Be especially mindful about the length of your sessions because this position is physically demanding for all dogs, and especially so for many Pigs Fly dogs. If you have a graceful Doberman or a slinky Border Collie, they can probably maintain this position for a long time without harm. If your dog is basically a cinderblock with a head attached, like mine are, fifteen minutes in this position could be injurious to their neck. Both for the physical well-being of the dog and the mental willingness to do the behavior, you are much better off to do just a few steps of attention walking each day or, better yet, several times a day.

Energize your dog's behavior with hot reinforcers. As we discussed in Chapter Seven, you need all kinds of reinforcers to keep your dog keen on attention walking. Also, you can take the forces that seem to be working against you and use them to your advantage this way. If there is something that you have noticed to be particularly distracting to your dog, use that as a hot reinforcer. For instance, if there is a spot that he keeps wanting to sniff, dig at, or generally investigate, let him do so in exchange for some attention walking.

Take it on the road very gradually. Graduate through the steps. Begin in your kitchen, and work your way up to your living room, back yard, front yard, your street, a new street, a hiking trail.

Yield on your requirements when you change something. You have built up this behavior systematically. First step anywhere in the magic circle, then add eye contact, then add closeness, then add staying in that position for a good stretch. If you ask for this carefully built behavior in a new context, don't expect or ask for all of those criteria at once. If you are, for instance, walking on a different route than you usually do, you may have to go back a step, or two steps. Perhaps you will reinforce if your dog is in the magic circle and looking at you, but not close. Maybe that is too much. Perhaps you will reinforce if your dog is in the magic circle at all. You might even have to go back to just free shaping some attention, but don't worry about it. When you have built up a behavior this way it is very durable and you will be able to piece the steps back together very quickly. Just go back to whatever your dog can do and work your way back up.

A relaxed trail walk with your best friend is one of the great pleasures in life. In contrast to attention walking, Ruby knows she can do whatever she likes, as long as she stays within the length of the leash.

Go Be a Dog
Casual Walking

OK, so now your dog knows how to do snappy attention walking. He has learned to pay attention to you and stay close in the face of all the interesting stuff in the world. You can get through a crowd with a bag of groceries in one hand and your dog's leash in the other. Now we can teach "just be a dog" walking.

When casual walking, your dog can be in any position relative to you so long as the leash is not tight. He is free to stop and sniff or do his business, but he has to come along with you when you start moving.

Shape. By now, your dog probably is conditioned to stay pretty close to you when you are walking. Now, just put the leash on and start walking. Depending on whether your dog is a "puller" or a "planter," we will approach the walk slightly differently.

For pullers: The fact that your dog is pulling tells you that moving forward is something he wants to do very much. What does that mean to you as a trainer? Moving forward can be used as a reinforcer! So, use the opportunity to move forward the same way you use any other reinforcer like food or toys or opportunity

The rules of this game are simple—keep the leash loose, and you get to move forward. Tighten up the leash, and I will stop until you turn around and put some slack in the leash.

to play. If your dog will give you the behavior you want (slack leash) he gets the reinforcer (move forward.) If he does not give you the behavior you want (he pulls on the leash) he does not get the reinforcer (you stand still and keep him from going forward.) Follow these steps:

1. As long as your dog is with you in any position that you find acceptable, keep moseying around. The rules of this game are, so long as he is not pulling, he gets to walk.

2. If the leash gets tight, stop moving. Don't give your dog any verbal or physical cue or correction other than your cessation of motion. Be like a rock and stand there. You have to make a commitment never to move forward if your dog is pulling on the leash. The reinforcer is the opportunity to move forward. You give that reinforcer to your dog in exchange for keeping the leash loose.

3. The instant there is any slack in the leash, move forward. Make it very obvious to your dog what the key is to forward movement. So long as you are consistent, it will not take long at all for him to figure out that pulling does not pay.

For planters: If walking your dog is like dragging a cement lawn ornament, that means that standing in one place is more reinforcing than walking with you. That is because either: 1) he has physical problems that keep him from enjoying a walk; or 2) walking with you has not been a fun or rewarding experience in the past.

First rule out any physical problems. Have your vet examine your dog and do a full thyroid panel, check for tick borne diseases (which can lead to lethargy and severe lameness), injury, and lameness. Take a good look at your dog's physical condition. It is hard for your dog to want to walk when he is so fat that standing up is an effort. You should be able to feel your dog's ribs and he should have an hourglass shape when viewed from above. Also, be aware of your dog's natural physical limitations and do not drag him on long walks that are past his ability. A Border Collie might love to run with you for miles while you rollerblade along the boulevard, but you don't own a Border Collie. Dragging a Scottie behind you for miles when his little legs can barely keep up and his heart is screaming for you to stop is not the way to make your dog love walking!

Shape walking with you to be a fun and rewarding experience. The fact that you are there and breathing is not enough to pique his interest. Keep the picture of a happy dog trotting next to you in your mind and approximate that picture in small segments.

1. Start by reinforcing for attention

2. Take ONE step and reinforce your dog like crazy when he follows you. Be sure to reinforce him after he has followed you. If you lure him with food and toys before he offers to walk for you, then you are always going to have to bring food and toys with you on a walk and that's a drag.

3. After he will happily follow you for one step, adding two, three, five, and ten steps is a piece of cake. Follow the reinforcement schedules in the appendix and you will have a dog that walks along with you in no time.

Lots of playing at home is helpful, too. Anything that puts an association between following you and a good time in your dog's mind is going to increase your value to him and make him more likely to want to walk with you.

Add a cue. The only cue for a casual walk is the fact that your dog is connected to you by a leash and you are walking. If your dog is on a leash and you are walking and you have not told him otherwise, your dog will come to know he is free to do what he wants, so long as the leash stays loose

Frequent but short sessions. Although your goal is to be able to take a nice long walk with your dog, start with very short walks. Put him on a leash and take him out to the mailbox with you, or around the corner, or into your front yard, or over to your neighbor's house to return the wrench you borrowed. It is easier for both you and your dog to "get it right" on these short jaunts and they will serve as a foundation for long walks.

Energize your dog's behavior with hot reinforcers. Just as you did with attention walking, add hot reinforcers from time to time to keep things interesting.

Take it on the road very gradually. The usual protocol of gradually practicing the behavior in more and more stimulating environments applies to casual walking. In addition, be aware that "planter" dogs may be reluctant to walk because they are actually fearful of walking in public. You can inoculate your scared dog against his fears by introducing walking in public in tiny, easily digestible pieces. In this way you can desensitize him to his fears of the world. If you pull him along to a place where he is scared and make him walk, you run the risk of sensitizing him to the thing he is scared of and actually making it worse.

There is nothing fundamentally different about the way you train a fearful dog to walk versus a non-fearful dog. You do, however, have to monitor your dog's fear level and be very careful to stay within his envelope of comfort. Study up with the book or DVD *On Talking Terms With Dogs: Calming Signals* by Turid Rugaas (see Resources). Learn to read your dog and know when your dog is the tiniest bit

---

---

scared or stressed so you can back off. Only move on to walking in more "scary" places in teeny, tiny, steps. Your dog should never be reluctant to walk with you. Shape your dog to beg to be walked, not to tolerate being walked.

Yield on your requirements when you change something. When you are walking somewhere new or somewhere really interesting like a hiking trail, you may have to use a much higher rate of reinforcement to get your dog to walk with you. By now you know the drill—go back to the behaviors that your dog can do, and build your way back up to walking nicely along with you.

Nosy Parker
Touch/Target

These are great behaviors to teach and come in handy more often than you might imagine. **Touch** (as in touch your outstretched hand) is a fabulous way to control your dog's body position and field of vision at any time. For "mouthy" dogs it is a perfect way for them to interact with you without using their teeth. **Target** (as in touch his nose or paw to a specific target) is an excellent way of teaching your dog to work at a distance from you.

It is handy to be able to position your dog with the flick of a hand. Here, the owner's hand says, "Move over to my left side." Then, "No, wait. Move over to my right side."

If your dog will voluntarily put his head wherever you put your hand, his body will automatically follow, so a touch command has endless practical applications. Anytime you want to reposition your dog or turn him away from something distracting, simply ask him to touch your hand. For distractible or easily over-stimulated types, this is a great way to center them and get their attention back on you. Most dogs seem to like the nose touch and appear almost relieved when you ask for it in the midst of a very chaotic or distracting environment. For some reason, it is easy for dogs to ignore a plea for general attention, but very difficult for them to resist touching your hand when asked to do so.

The touch works very nicely to get a sniffing dog's nose off the ground and back up into your territory. If you were trying to take a walk with a reluctant and distracted Basset Hound whose nose is glued to the ground, you could ask him to jump up and touch your hand—at once getting his nose up off the ground and lighting a little fire under his tail with a fun movement.

Teaching your dog to touch an object like a large yogurt container lid with his nose ("targeting") is also a very useful behavior. Pigs Fly dogs seem to feel that if you have any influence over them at all, it only extends to a two foot diameter around you. Beyond that, all bets are off and your Pigs Fly dog is unlikely to honor any requests. By training your dog to go out to targets, you can teach him the important concept that you do still exist, even though you are four feet away. Also, if you want to shape your dog to do something like go lie down on his bed, or go to his crate from anywhere in the house, teaching your dog to target is a great way to get him used to the concept of moving away from you.

Shape the touch. Here are the steps to shape a touch:

1. Extend your empty hand, palm up near the dog's face. Be very still—do not move your hand toward his nose at all. The behavior you want to isolate and click is your dog's head moving towards your hand, not your dog allowing you to hit him in the nose with your hand. He will almost certainly check out your hand with his nose. As soon as he moves his nose towards your hand, click/treat out of the other hand. Within a few clicks he will be boinking his nose on your hand.

2. Once your dog is very deliberately boinking your hand with his nose, you can start moving your hand around. At first, move your hand so that your dog only has to turn his head,

Once your dog learns how to jump up for a hand touch, they often enjoy it so much that you can use it as a reinforcer.

then move your hand so that he has to take a step, then two steps, and so forth. Now you can position your dog anywhere you like by just moving your hand!

3. Gradually move your hand over your dog's head until your dog will reach his nose up and touch your hand.

4. Now gradually hold your hand higher and higher over his head and shape a "leap up into the air" behavior. This bouncing motion is a lot of fun and very stimulating. You can mix quick nose touches in with loose leash walking to rev up the activity. The touch behavior is a good example of a cold behavior that can quickly become so hot that it can be used to reinforce other cold behaviors!

Pig Tale
Kody the Pharaoh Hound had a nose that his owner described as "almost prehensile." Poking something with his nose was a huge pleasure for Kody and the touch game was one of his favorites.

Shape the target.

1. Place a lid, like one from a large yogurt container, down on the floor in front of your dog. He will almost certainly investigate with his nose. Click and treat him if he does. If your dog is more foot-oriented and he would prefer to paw at the target, that is OK, too. Pick either the nose touch or the paw whack and always reinforce it.

If your dog can learn to run away from you and target something, you can use that to teach him to his mat, go to his crate, go out the door, or any other behavior that requires him to turn away from you and go in the direction you indicate.

2. Place the target further and further away from you and your dog will run away from you to go touch it. You will eventually be able to send your dog away in any direction and he will run out to find the target.

Add a cue. Once your dog is clearly offering to touch your outstretched hand or the target, you can add the cue: "touch" for a hand touch, and "target" for touching or pawing a lid target.

Frequent but short sessions. Touch and target are not complicated behaviors and you don't have to spend long training them to for your dog "get it."

The hand touch is especially easy to incorporate into your daily life. When ever you want your dog near you, throw down your hand and ask him to touch—it's a fun game.

Energize your dog's behavior with hot reinforcers. Mix in your hot reinforcers for targets and touches. You may soon find that a hand touch has become a reinforcer, itself.

Take it on the road very gradually. As we discussed earlier, the hand touch is a valuable tool when you are out on the road. Your hand touch will be a "re-centering" activity with which you can get your dog's attention and control his position. It is such an easy activity that you can usually get your dog to do it even when he is too distracted to do any other behavior. If you are out on the road and you can't even get your dog to touch your hand, your dog is probably in over his head and need to go back to a less stimulating environment.

Simple Math
Recall

Getting a Pigs Fly dog to come when called, especially with distractions, is one of the most challenging things you will ever do. When you call a Sheltie, he will generally snap to attention and zoom into you as fast as his cute little legs will carry him. When you call your dog, what happens? He runs a complex risk-benefit analysis which involves taking an extensive inventory of all the known interesting things multiplied by the

Successfully training a Pigs Fly dog to come when called is a real achievement!

promising possibilities he can explore if he remains at liberty, versus the fact that you would be very happy, or at least not too angry, if he came to you. Hmm. Wonder how that equation is going to work out?

A lot of people want to know why their dog won't come when called. To me it is much more mystifying why some breeds of dogs generally DO come when called. On one side of the balance sheet is the lure of everything interesting, fun, and good in the world, and on the other side is "You". What does You mean to your dog? Biddable dogs seem to be born with an abnormally high opinion of You. It is just not natural to want to give up liberty and all the fun that goes with it at the drop of a hat, simply for the chance to be near a human. There has to have been some very strong genetic selection for this trait. Your Pigs Fly dog is not equipped with the "come when called" gene. Until we isolate that gene and learn how to splice it onto the "Come? Whaddayoucrazy?" gene, we will have to rely on training and conditioning to build up the value of You to your dog.

Piggy Pointer

It is dismaying to many dog owners that their dog prefers to do almost anything rather than come when called. They think their dog "should" come when called because they, the handler, say so, without any further incentive. Our cultural ideal is of a dog loyal and devoted, adoring eyes shining as he gazes lovingly at his master. Forget it! Yes, there are some breeds of dog that are closer to that cultural ideal than others, but Pigs Fly breeds do not usually personify this type. Let go of the emotional baggage of "should," "ought to," and "because I say so," and get back to training behaviors. It is the only way you will ever succeed.

So, let's say that All The Interesting Stuff In The World is on one side of the scale, and You are on the other. All The Interesting Stuff weighs about 100 pounds, and You weigh, oh, let's see…about 3 ounces. Really. If you call your dog to you and give him one piece of food one time, you just added approximately one ounce to your side. If you gave him a super-hot reinforcer, you might add nine ounces to Your side. If you doled out 100 tiny pieces of food in rapid succession when he came to you, that might be worth about twelve ounces. If you did all of those things, it would add up to an extra pound or two on your side and you would have made some good progress towards a reliable recall.

Now, if you call your dog to you and yell at him because he was digging your flower bed, you just put another pound on the scale on the All The Interesting Stuff side. Although you have added a pound to your side of the scale through previous reinforcement, the outside world now weighs about 101 pounds and you are back to square one. Are you beginning to get a feel for the enormity of reinforcement that is necessary to build a recall? It is simple math:

The history of reinforcement for coming when called

Minus

The level of excitement/stimulation/novelty of the environment

Equals

The likelihood that your dog will come when called.

So, now that you have the formula, let's begin to work on shaping it to your advantage.

Shape. I am going to give you two shaping games to play with your dog to teach him a recall. You can use one or both of them, depending on your circumstances and which one appeals to you. The more recall games you play with your dog, the better his recall will be.

Cheese Ball Recalls

1. Get yourself some of those day-glow cheese balls that come in a plastic barrel. You could also use tortellini or anything else that is large enough and of a bright enough color to be seen when tossed in the ground, but I call it "cheese ball recalls" because tortellini does not rhyme with recall!

2. Show your dog the cheese ball, and toss it away from you. If sees it, he will run after it.

3. While your dog is busy eating the cheese ball, run away as fast as you can while still keeping an eye on your dog (a tricky maneuver, but you will get better at it with practice). Your dog will be attracted to you by your running, and he will start moving towards you. Click as soon as he moves in your direction, and give him a cheese ball out of your hand as soon as he reaches you.

4. Throw another cheese ball away from you and start over.

5. Although you should first click any motion towards you, gradually start clicking your dog for being closer and closer to you, until you are clicking only when he actually reaches you.

Piggy Pointer
If your dog stops dead in his tracks when he hears the click and does not continue running in towards you, don't worry. The idea is to mark the initial act of moving towards you, and you succeeded in doing that. You can show him the treat or toy or whatever you have to offer him to lure him in after the click.

See how much excitement this game generates? While your dog is busy eating the cheese ball you have thrown, run like heck. The faster you can run, the more exciting it will be for your dog and the easier for him to learn the recall.

Pass the Dog Game (you will need a friend's help):

1. You and your friend sit on the floor, about eight feet away from each other. You are both armed with clickers and food. Have your friend hold your dog facing you.

2. How you handle the next step depends on your dog. Say his name. If your dog alerts to you and is looking eagerly towards you and/or straining towards you, your friend should release your dog. As soon as your dog starts moving towards you, click. Don't wait until he is actually near you. Click the very first footstep of moving towards you. Your dog will run to you to get his treat. Note that if your dog was not looking at you or straining to get to you, you can make kissing noises, tap your fingers on the ground, or if all else fails, you can show him the treats or a toy. Whatever you have to do, make sure that, when your friend releases your dog, he is going to start moving in your direction.

3. Now do the same thing, but with you restraining your dog and your friend clicking and treating.

Another game that teaches dogs that it is FUN to come when called. Begin by sitting close to each other as in this picture, but quickly increase the distance the dog has to travel to get to the next person.

4. Do this back and forth a few times, and gradually start clicking your dog as he gets closer and closer to you, instead of clicking for just beginning to move towards you. Eventually, you will click only when your dog actually reaches you.

5. Gradually move further away from your friend. How far apart you go in this step will depend on your dog, his size, and his age, but fifteen to twenty feet is an average goal.

6. If you can get more than one person to play the game with you, that is very helpful. Be random about who the dog is to go to next—sometimes the person next to him, sometimes the person across from him, etc.

Add a cue. When you have gotten to the point where you are clicking your dog for actually coming close to you, you can add a cue. If you have been playing "pass the dog" and "cheese ball recalls," and you know for sure that your dog is going to come to you because he has just done it a several times in a row in the same location that you are in now, you can add the cue just as your dog is turning towards you. At this point it should be easy to predict when your dog will come to you so that you can add your cue before the behavior right off the bat.

It is especially important that your recall cue sounds the same each time. Use the word "come" and say it in a high, clipped, voice—almost a chirp. It is good to say it that way because that staccato sound will carry over a long distance. Also, dogs tend to be drawn in and motivated to move faster by short, high pitched sounds and kept away and/or slowed down by long, low pitched ones.

As with your dog's name, the recall cue must be a sacred sound that only ever has good associations for your dog. Never call your dog to you and then scold him or punish him in any way. Go and get him if whatever follows might not be an activity he likes. You may see a Cattle Dog coming to his owner, looking very unhappy because he knows there is a good chance he might be getting a bath or a toenail clip or a trip to the vet. The Cattle Dog is so reinforced by his owner's mere presence, that he will overcome his abhorrence of whatever activity is planned so he can comply with his owner's wishes. Your dog will never do that. If your Pigs Fly Dog thought you were calling him to do one of those stinky activities, he would either run away or stand in the middle of the yard with a bubble above his head that reads, "Yeah, right." If you want your dog to come to you, you are going to have make sure that your recall cue always means something good for your dog.

Sometimes you are going to need to call your dog when what follows is not the best thing in the world. For instance, you have to leave for work so you call your dog in from the yard so you can put him in his crate. Make sure that, even if you going to put him in his crate, he gets a really fantastic jackpot of reinforcers for coming to you when called. Give him food, toys, play—whatever floats his boat. If you make the reinforcer strong enough, it will break the association between being called in and being put in his crate for the day.

Frequent but short sessions. Make sure you end your formal sessions while your dog is still really hyped up about the recall. Just a few recalls a day is all you need to build a strong behavior. Make it a point to call your dog to you a few times a day around the house and give him some incredible reinforcer. The surprise factor helps cement the recall in your dog's mind as something great.

Energize your dog's behavior with hot reinforcers. Coming to you when called is the single most important behavior your dog will ever learn, and you should lay on the reinforcements as thickly and as creatively as possible. Great food is a good reinforcer, but if your dog's number one passion in life is a squeaky toy, make sure he gets it sometimes for coming to you. Make sure he does not see the squeaky toy before he comes to you, or he will only ever come when you are holding the toy. Surprise is the key element here.

Take it on the road very gradually. Refer back to the formula in the beginning of this section: The history of reinforcement for coming when called, minus the level of excitement/stimulation/novelty of the environment, equals the likelihood that your dog will come when called. Slant things in your favor by either adding to the history of reinforcement, or diminishing the excitement/stimulation/novelty of the environment. Improve the history of reinforcement by more repetitions with great reinforcers. Diminish the allure of everything else by limiting your dog's scope—either a boring venue like a kitchen or a familiar back yard, or a leash that limits your dog's access to fun stuff.

For instance, if you want to have your dog come when called if you are in the kitchen and your dog is sleeping on his bed, you might only have to call him into the kitchen and give him his dinner one time for him to come promptly every time you call him in that situation. Sleeping on a bed is mundane and getting dinner is about the most exciting thing that happens in many dogs' lives. OK, so you have that covered. What about your back yard? Well, there are squirrels and smells and fences to bark over—you had better have reinforced that dog dozens of times with really good stuff for coming when called before attempting that particular recall. If you are going to take your dog to a park or on a trail and let him off leash, you may need literally years of substantial reinforcement history of coming when called. In the meantime you may need to make sure your dog is safely on a long leash before you can try that stunt.

A note about Pigs Fly dogs and recalls. I have no doubt that some breeds of dogs can be trained to reliably stay with you off leash. I harbor a "cheater" dog, an Australian Cattle Dog who I can take anywhere off leash. He can be chasing something down at top speed and will stop and turn so quickly when I call him that it looks like an optical illusion. In twenty-four years of having Bull Terriers, I have never owned or seen one that I would trust indefinitely off leash. I know lots of people that do let their Bull Terriers go off leash all the time, but they do not have the kind of recall that I consider acceptable for that and they are taking a big risk. Thirty foot leashes are cheap and easy to find—most places in the United States have leash laws anyway, so you are better off to observe them.

Yield on your requirements when you change something. Keep in mind that a recall in your back yard is not a recall in a crowded park with lots of dogs and people around. Be realistic in your expectations, and manage your dog by keeping him on leash if you don't think he will come when called. If you do take him off leash away from home, make sure that you don't let him get too far away. Recall him early and often, and reinforce him generously for coming!

It is so important that you painstakingly build a solid recall that I could devote an entire chapter, or even a small book, to that alone. I have given you what you need to know in order to teach a great recall. As a visual study aid for this behavior, I highly recommend that you view Leslie Nelson's *Really Reliable Recall* DVD. Leslie has done a beautiful job laying out a step by step program for teaching a reliable recall under any circumstances, and the DVD is very helpful in showing just how to set up and proof a perfect recall.

A Couple More Handy Behaviors

Before we move on to dealing with problem behaviors, you will need to shape two more simple behaviors. By now you should understand SAFETY training, so I am only going to give you some tips on how to shape them:

Back Up

"Back up" is a highly underrated behavior with many uses. It is surprising that most basic dog training books do not include back up as part of their canon of basic pet obedience. Any time you want your dog out of the way, you can ask him to back up. If he is crowding the door, you can ask him to back up. If you are coming into the yard and he is pushing to escape through the gate when you open it, you can ask him to back up. If your dog is a show dog you can ask him to back up instead of turning in a circle to re-stack. As you will see in the following section, back up is also an indispensable behavior for dealing with pushy or aggressive dogs.

Here is a way to shape it. First, you can try to catch your dog in the act of taking a step back and then click it. Most dogs, when thinking or slightly frustrated, will take a step back. Also, most dogs will take a step back just before barking at you.

If you want to speed the process along, you can step into your dog slightly. Just step into him enough until he shifts his weight back slightly and click that—you can build on that to taking steps backwards. You have to be quick with the click because when you step into your dog, his tendency will be to sit down—if you are slow with the click you will find yourself clicking a sit.

You can step into your dog a little in order to help him back up. If he sits, do not click and try to be faster with your click next time. Otherwise you are teaching him to "Sit" rather than to "Back up."

Go to Your Crate/Go to Your Mat

Your dog should willingly go to his crate any time you ask him to.

Your dog needs a crate. It should be his cozy little den where he can go chill out when he needs some down time. It is his room and he should enjoy going into it when the situation demands. Just like people, dogs do not want to be locked up in their rooms for extended periods of time, but there is nothing better than having your own room to go to when you feel like it or it is time to sleep or be alone. A crate will keep your dog out of trouble when you need some down time. Life is just hard when you can't put your dog away sometimes.

Piggy Pointer
If, for some reason, a crate is out of the question, buy an exercise pen and make that your dog's special spot.

I want my dogs to love going into their crates, not just tolerate it. When someone who does not care for dogs is at the door and I have five dogs loose and I want to get them all put away quickly, it is nice to have dogs that will run to their crates without hesitation. It would be troublesome to drag each dog into his crate, so I make sure that they will fly into them eagerly. You are going to shape going into the crate much the same way that you played the cardboard box game:

1. Walk your dog over to an open crate and just stand there. Click for any glance at the crate and then feed the dog inside the crate.

2. Now hold out for a foot step towards the crate.

3. Next hold out for one foot in the crate.

4. Gradually shape your dog to go into the crate on his own. It will not take long until your dog is running ahead of you into his crate on cue.

You can teach your dog to go lie down on a mat or dog bed the same way. Shape your dog to go to the mat/bed, and then shape him to lie down on it. I keep a dog bed next to my desk and periodically reinforce my dogs for lying down quietly on it while I am working.

Shaping your dog step by step to go his crate.

You Both Should be Having Fun
How to Take Your Dog for a Walk

Now that you have all these foundation behaviors in place on your dog, you are ready to hit the trail and have some fun with your buddy. Nothing is a better bonding and training experience than a walk with your well-trained dog. Exercise can be very relaxing and healthy. If you have trained your foundation behaviors well, the pleasant associations you and your dog make while out for a walk will contribute greatly towards building a strong relationship between you. In this section, you will learn how to take a walk with your dog and make it an enjoyable experience for both of you.

Do you really need someone to tell you how to take your dog for a walk? Put a leash on and go out the door, right? As long as you can figure out how to make him stop pulling on the leash, everything's okey-dokey, isn't that so? You owners of Pigs Fly kinda dogs know it is not so simple. You will only get that nice enjoyable walk if you have mastered most of the foundation behaviors in this chapter. Have you succeeded in training the foundation behaviors? Great! Let's see how you can use them on a walk.

Taking a walk is more than just dragging a dog along or keeping him from dragging you along. Think of it as a cross-training workout where you get to test and try all of the behaviors you have trained in different contexts. By using and reinforcing all of your foundation behaviors everytime you take a walk, you make the walk more interactive and fun for you and your dog. Your dog learns that you are a fun person to be with and that hanging out near you is full of unexpected good surprises and opportunities to earn rewards. Here is how you might use all the foundation behaviors you have trained on a typical walk.

1. Leaving the yard—Back Up at the gate.

2. Sit and Stay at the gate.

3. Come through the gate.

4. Don't want your leash to wrap around the fence post? Attention Walk past that.

5. Casual Walking on the trail.

5. Pop quiz—Come!

6. Back to Casual Walking.

7. Bicycle coming through! Come! Move off trail and Sit-Stay with Attention.

8. Back to Casual Walking.

9. Your shoe came untied. Down-Stay, while you tie your shoe.

10. Pedestrians approaching—Come!

11. Your dog may be friendly, but you don't want him to pester the pedestrians with affection. Attention walk past them.

12. You don't want your dog walking through that high grass with ticks in it so move him to your other side with a Hand Touch.

13. Eeeew, dead groundhog. Attention Walk past that one.

14. Back home—Go to Your Crate.

15. A good dog is a tired dog—be sure to reinforce him for Lying Down quietly after his walk.

Congratulations! You have done something that was probably previously impossible for you and your dog to do together. Pigs have flown! A jackpot for both of you!

Training with rewards is the way to get your dog to walk politely and love it. This previously unruly dog is now a joy to walk with.

10
ABCs of Living With a Pigs Fly Dog
Problem Behaviors

Now that you have taught your dog foundation behaviors, gotten him passionate about offering them, and practiced them everywhere, you are equipped to tackle any behavior complaint you have with your dog. You may wonder how this is possible. You just want to make your dog stop doing "bad" things and stop now! "Gee thanks," you might be thinking, "you showed me how to teach my dog to offer all kinds of behaviors, but I don't want behaviors and I don't care if my dog is operant, I just want him to stop jumping on me!" Let's see how you can use the power of your foundation behaviors to crowd out the behaviors you do not like.

Humans tend to think that Pigs Fly dogs are "bad" because they frequently indulge in activities that we don't like, such as digging, barking, pulling, tearing apart upholstered furniture, etc. Our Pigs Fly dogs are simply doing what is natural to them. They lack the abstract mind of a philosopher necessary to have a concept of right and wrong. Get your tattoo gun out, because I want you to tattoo these two concepts on your arm:

> When it comes to dogs, there are no "good" or "bad" behaviors. There are only "behaviors" and the dog is born thinking they are all equal.

And also this:

> Two behaviors cannot occupy the same space at the same time.

> If your dog is doing a behavior of which you approve, he cannot be doing a behavior of which you disapprove.

If you can grasp these two concepts, your life will go much more smoothly. Dogs have no sense of morality or shame. What they do have is a huge self-interest and they will do whatever it takes to promote their cause. If waiting politely for you to open the door and let them out pays dividends, and trying to blast past you to get out does not, they will opt for waiting politely. You don't need to be a doggie Freudian to figure this out—all you have to do is let go of your preconceived notion that rushing past you is a "bad" behavior, and train the behavior that you like in its place.

Now that your dog is operant and will offer you his nice little portfolio of foundation behaviors, we can shape him to do anything, including behave the way you would like him to. Let's look at how you can use what you have taught your dog so far to solve any problem behavior—all you need to know is your ABCs, a concept first introduced by trainers Marian and Bob Bailey (see Resources).

A is for Antecedent

Don't be put off if you have no idea what antecedent means—it is not exactly a term we use every day. It's just a term for something that comes before something else.

Dogs do not do things in a vacuum. Despite what people think, dogs almost never do anything "without warning" or "out of nowhere." Every behavior was prompted by something, be it a sight, a sound, a physical sensation, or a situation. Some examples that you might be familiar with are:

1. A ringing doorbell—prompts a dog to bark.

2. An open refrigerator door—prompts a dog to poke his head in and grab something.

3. Running, screaming, children—prompts a dog to nip.

4. A new person approaching—prompts a dog to jump on them.

The ringing doorbell, the open refrigerator door, the running children, and the approaching new person all prompted a behavior in the dog. Something that prompts behavior in this way is called an **antecedent**.

B is for Behavior

Every single moment your dog is breathing, he is doing some kind of behavior. In the examples above, barking, stealing food, jumping, and nipping are some all-too-familiar behaviors for most Pigs Fly dog owners. But did you know that all the good things your dog does are behaviors, too? Lying down quietly on a mat is a behavior. Sitting politely to be patted is a behavior. Even sleeping is a behavior. So, the B in ABC stands for **behavior**.

C is for Consequence

Well, why does any particular antecedent prompt a particular behavior? Why should a ringing doorbell make a dog bark? Why should an open refrigerator door make a dog stick his head in and steal something? What sustains or diminishes a behavior is the consequence of that behavior. If the consequence is something the dog likes, he will do the behavior more and more. If it is something he does not like, he will do the behavior less and less. So the C in ABC stands for **consequence**.

Now we will go down the list of ABC situations that grieve the average dog owner, de-install the troublesome behaviors and insert a new behavior from our portfolio of foundation behaviors. Your operant dog will get it in no time that, in order to earn a good consequence, he needs to respond to the antecedent, with a behavior that pays. Your dog can only do one behavior at a time, so when we install the new behaviors, the old, troublesome, ones go away. Here is the process:

1. Figure out the antecedent. What is the event, thing, or situation is prompting your dog to engage in the behavior you do not like? If you can't figure out what the antecedent is at first, just make a note of what was happening right before he did the "bad" thing. If you do that a few times, a pattern will jump out at you and you will see what the antecedent is.

2. You then have two options regarding your dog's behavior:

   a. Train an alternate behavior. Think of a behavior that you would like your dog to do instead of the "bad" behavior and start training him to automatically perform the "good" behavior in response to the antecedent, or

   b. If you can't train, manage. If you don't have the time right now to train an alternate behavior, or if the behavior is one that is very dangerous or difficult (or even impossible) to train out, manage the situation by removing your dog to another place, like his crate. You will keep him from doing the "bad" thing. If you take the time to figure out the antecedents, you can literally make sure that your dog never does anything wrong because you can stop him before he does.

3. Make the consequence of doing the right thing very reinforcing. Make sure that your dog gets rewarded for doing the "right" thing and he will always choose to do the "right" thing. Incidentally, this will also be very reinforcing for you, too. It is a tiring downer to be constantly angry and nagging at another member of your household. Your own outlook on life will be much happier if you are looking for ways to reinforce your dog for good things instead of being a warden who is on the lookout for bad behaviors to punish.

I have selected the nine problem behaviors that, in my experience, Pigs Fly dog owners complain about most, but, as you can see, you can use the ABC principle to change any behavior.

1. Jumping up on people

2. Going crazy when the doorbell rings

3. Nipping

4. Restlessness around the house

5. Barking

6. Chewing

7. Charging doors

8. Housetraining issues

9. Aggression

I Would Shake Your Hand if I Had Opposable Thumbs
Jumping on People

Here is the classic ABC of dogs jumping on people:

A. Person approaches.

B. Dog jumps on them.

C. Person pushes, yells at, "knees," or strikes dog.

If you are reading this section, I am 90% certain that you have tried getting your dog not to jump on you in this way and it has not worked. Although you are certain that the treatment you have been giving your dog in exchange for jumping on you should be punishing enough to stop the behavior, it doesn't do so reliably. You have either have had limited success, or found that, although you might keep your dog from jumping on you, he will still jump on strangers, especially small and weak strangers. Let's examine the reasons for this.

Think about puppies greeting an adult dog. What do they do? They jump up and lick the face of the adult, saying, "I am small, will not hurt you, and I want to be loved and not harmed by you." A normal adult dog will not harm a puppy or dog that offers that behavior. So, the "jumping in greeting" ABC that your dog comes pre-equipped with is this:

A. Adult dog approaches.

B. Puppy jumps up and licks face and mouth of adult dog.

C. Adult dog offers some pleasant greeting behavior in exchange—regurgitates food, plays with puppies or engages puppies in another non-aggressive interaction.

Can you see how confusing it is for your dog when you do bad stuff to him for jumping on you? Your dog sees a new person. Your dog offers the absolutely correct and appropriate submissive behavior of jumping up and pawing at the stranger. The dog is doing what he is hard-wired to do. In evolutionary terms, it was the correct behavior to offer under the circumstances. We humans, however, being retarded when it comes to dog language, fail to be appeased by this behavior and yell at/strike/jerk on the collar of or give a knee to the dog. Now the dog thinks, "Holy smokes, I must not have given a strong enough submissive signal! Better try it again, only this time I am going to get really frantically submissive so there can be no mistake!" The dog jumps faster and harder at you in an attempt to display his submissiveness. Lo and behold, a vicious circle of futile violence and misunderstanding is born.

Yeah, you may be able to punish the dog enough that he is actually afraid of people and will not come near. As we noted previously, however, Pigs Fly dogs often seem to be unimpressed by usual levels of physical punishment, and you may have to dig deep and get quite rough to suppress the jumping behavior. Furthermore, you will not have taught him an "acceptable to humans" behavior that he can do in response to the antecedent of an approaching person. You only taught him that an approaching human is a cue for something very unpleasant so he had better stay away. Approaching stranger equals something very unpleasant—need I add that the seeds of aggression towards people might be planted in this way?

It gets worse. Because your dog has not learned what to do when meeting people, he will still jump on people if he thinks he can do so without being subject to "the treatment." This is why, even though you thought you had punished this behavior out of your dog, the "jumping on people" behavior will reappear spontaneously with new people, especially small or weak people who might not be able to deliver sufficiently strong physical aversives to stop the dog from doing it.

OK, now it's time for you to put on your thinking cap and come up with a creative solution. The antecedent is a person approaching your dog. Instead of the behavior of jumping on them, what would you like your dog to do? "Not jump on them" is not a behavior—you have to pick something specific that your dog can do, not what you do not want him to do. How about this?

A. Person approaches.

B. Dog sits automatically.

C. Person greets and pats/pays attention to the dog.

Wouldn't that be pleasant? Here is a plan for teaching it:

1. Have your dog sit, on leash. A friend approaches and walks around at whatever distance they need to in order for the dog to stay seated and not jump up. This might be 100 feet, but you need to work inside the dog's comfort level. Click treat for dog remaining seated.

2. Build up by increments to where the person is standing in front of the dog—as long as the dog remains seated he is click/treated and receives attention and patting from the friend. If the dog breaks position, the treats go away and your friend turns away. It will not take long at all until a person approaching becomes a cue for you dog to sit politely and wait to be patted.

3. Remember why your dog is jumping in the first place—he wants attention. You will get the best results if you ask everyone to please pat your dog while he is sitting nicely. It will prove to him that sitting nicely is the key to getting what he wants—attention.

Nicky is obviously excited to see a friend, but he has learned that the way he will get attention is to sit down politely and wait to be petted.

4. Alternatively, you can have your friend approach and, as she approaches, give the dog the cue to sit and click/treat. After 20 or so reps, your dog just might start offering the behavior on his own. If the dog breaks the position at anytime do not say no or offer any correction. Ignore the dog for a little while, repeat the sit command, and try again. Ignore what you don't want and reinforce what you want.

Now greetings with your dog can be a bonding experience instead of a clash of wills. Even the smallest or weakest person is safe around a dog that has been trained this way. Simple, elegant, and it actually works.

Piggy Pointer

You can also stop your dog from offering appeasing behaviors like jumping up on you instantly by offering the correct calming signals. If you simply stand or sit up very straight, cross your arms, and turn your head away with your nose held high in a snooty attitude, your dog will almost instantly calm down. I first learned this bit of dog management when reading Patricia McConnell's *The Other End of The Leash* (see Resources). Obsessive licking (dog licking you, that is) can also be stopped in this way. Dogs respond so well to correct body language in humans that if you could teach everyone who comes in contact with your dog to behave "correctly," you would never have any problem with your dog jumping up at all. The reality is, however, that not only do people not respond in dog-appropriate ways, most people (especially children) will unwittingly and unerringly display the most antagonistic/arousing behavior possible. There is nothing for it but to teach your dog to respond to this craziness in a way that the human world will find acceptable.

All you need is the correct body language to keep a dog from jumping up on you.

Disarming Your Dog's Alarm System
Going Crazy When the Doorbell Rings

Many people are bothered by a dog that goes ballistic when the doorbell rings. I think barking at the doorbell is a useful behavior, but some people would prefer that their dogs not bark in that situation, and I respect that. For those of you who so desire, I'll show you how you can change this behavior.

This is what you probably have now:

   A. Doorbell rings.

   B. Dog goes crazy barking.

   C. New person comes in the door (Very Exciting!).

Now think for a moment. What would you like to see under "B" instead of "Dog goes crazy barking?" You could pick anything—i.e. down in the kitchen, come over to you and nose touch your hand, sit quietly in the middle of the living room and wait to be greeted. How about "dog runs to his crate and lies down?" Wouldn't that be nice? The crate behavior is great because you can also manage his greeting behaviors that way. Until he is fully trained to sit politely in greeting, you can close him in his crate and keep him from practicing the "wrong" behavior. Right now the doorbell predicts the entrance of a new person or stranger, and that is pretty hot stuff as far as your dog is concerned. You need to re-program the doorbell to predict "a fabulous treat/toy is going to appear in your crate." Here is how you will do it:

1. Stand with your dog near his crate.

2. Have a friend ring the doorbell—you may need to have your dog on leash to keep him from bolting, at first.

3. Toss something very high value into your dog's crate—a favorite toy or food. Click him when he goes in and give him some more treats.

4. Alternatively, if you have shaped a "go to your crate" behavior, you can send your dog to his crate and then feed/give him a toy.

Please note that this behavior is not "doorbell rings and dog gets dragged forcibly to his crate." This is the dog taking action in response to the doorbell ringing. The ringing doorbell has to predict something pleasant in exchange for a "good" behavior, and being dragged hither on a leash is not pleasant.

How many repetitions of pairing the doorbell with going to the crate will be necessary until the doorbell truly is a cue for your dog to go to his crate will depend entirely on your dog and how many times and how intensely he has practiced barking at the doorbell in the past. Eventually you will have:

A. Doorbell rings.

B. Dog runs to his crate.

C. Lots of great treats or toys (Yea!).

Love Hurts
Nipping

Nipping is a trickier than reacting to the doorbell ringing or jumping on people behaviors because the antecedents for nipping are not always clear until you start paying attention to them. First, you will need to note when your dog nips you and what was happening immediately before the nip, and that will vary somewhat from dog to dog. I am going to use a common example of a dog that nips because he is excited to see his owner.

1. Owner comes home.

2. Dog nips.

3. Owner shoves/pushes/yells at dog (how antagonizing!).

Piggy Pointer
The nipping I am talking about here is the kind of completely non-aggressive nudgey nipping that a rambunctious or excited dog might do. If your dog is freezing or growling before he nips, or if you are in any way in doubt and think he might be nipping out of aggression, that is a situation that requires professional help. Please find a qualified dog trainer to help you.

Now, remember your dog does not have opposable thumbs or arms that wrap around you. He can't hold your hand or hug you. His main means of touching you is with his mouth. Although it hurts you, chances are he is just trying to communicate with you in a way that comes naturally to him. So, when you are thinking about selecting a substitute behavior for nipping from your list of foundation behaviors, which one do you think might keep your skin intact, but still give your dog a chance to interact with you the way he wants to? How about a touch behavior?

A. Walk in your door or into the room where your dog is.

B. Throw your hand down, say "touch" and click and treat.

C. If you find yourself in a situation where you don't have a clicker or food on you, lavish attention on your dog after he touches your hand.

Now you will have:

A. Owner comes home and extends hand.

B. Dog touches nose to hand.

C. Owner greets and rewards dog.

(You may have to repeat the touch-cycle many times during each interaction.)

Soon your dog will be happily boinking your hand with his nose when he sees you. For dogs who are generally over the top with excitement, a hand touch can be used to center them again at anytime.

If your dog is nipping you at other times, you have to do your homework with the antecedents. Figure out how to predict when he might nip, and put your hand down and ask for a touch well before your dog actually does nip you. Usually, a dog that is about to get into an excited nipping sequence will have changes in his breathing and body posture that you can learn to read if you are observant. The whole key is to learn the earliest possible predictor for nipping and ask for a hand touch at that time, instead. If you can predict when your dog will nip before he himself has even fully formed the idea of nipping you, you can completely re-program his thought process and make hand touching his default behavior instead of nipping.

Here is another common nipping ABC story:

1. Children playing rough, screaming, and running around.

2. Dog runs around with the children and eventually gets wound up enough to start nipping.

3. Children wail and scream really loudly and sound like wounded prey animals. (How exciting!)

My first advice in this situation is, don't ever let it happen. In this ABC story, you need to watch out for the antecedent and manage the situation so that your dog does not engage in rough play. If your children are going to be playing rough games, especially games where the children might hurt each other and start screaming, let your dog hang out with you while the kids play. Don't leave your dog unsupervised with rowdy children. Your dog may either join in the fun and nip, or "defend" one of the children from another aggressive child. You can't blame him in either case, but he can wind up paying for it with his life. Parental management is called for.

Notwithstanding that advice, it is a good thing to teach a dog an alternate and acceptable behavior in response to children behaving wildly, in case you make a mistake and leave your dog outside with some wild kids. How about this?

A. Children playing rough, screaming, and running around.

B. Dog comes to you when you call (you have been standing by, monitoring the situation).

C. Dog receives a big reward of treats and praise.

Now unruly children become a predictor for good things if your dog leaves them alone and comes to you. Again, you should never rely on your dog to automatically leave hyper-stimulated children alone. It is not fair to the dog or the children to expect that. However, at least if you practice this ABC enough, your dog will not escalate his behavior as quickly and he will be (with enough practice) willing to come to you even under the extreme provocation of wailing children.

Regarding the interactions of children and dogs, I cannot recommend strongly enough that you visit www.doggonesafe.com. This is an incredibly interesting and informative website dedicated solely to dog bite prevention. They offer games and other interactive materials that will help you and your children learn how to safely interact with dogs.

Chill Out, Please!
Restlessness Around the House

It is a big pain to have a dog that never calms down. Sometimes wouldn't you give anything to have your dog lie down quietly next to you and relax? Here is a news flash:

Lying down quietly is a behavior.

An operant dog will offer lying down quietly just as he will offer any other behavior.

You can free shape quietness around the house just like you shaped all the other behaviors you have taught your dog. Catch your dog in the act of being calm, and reinforce the heck out of it. The difference is with a sit or a down you might effectively teach a behavior in one or two sessions, calmness around the house is a life project that you reinforce persistently over time. You will see some immediate results when you start reinforcing calm behaviors, but your dog will become more and more civilized as you make reinforcing your dog's calmness a habit.

In order to get calmness around the house, use a two-pronged approach.

1. Do an ABC list for when your dog is calm. No dog is wild every single second of his existence. Find the calm periods and see what led up to them. If you know what antecedents lead to calm behavior, you can stack the deck in your favor for more calm behavior by making sure that those antecedents happen more often.

2. Next, do an ABC list for when your dog is wild. Once you know what predicts unruly behavior, you can manage the situation so that your dog doesn't have a chance to practice going wild in the house.

Persistent behaviors are habits, and if dog practices calm behaviors instead of wild behaviors, he will eventually get into the habit of acting calm around the house.

You need to observe your dog's behavior and come up with your own ABC lists, but here are some common examples:

For Calm Behaviors:

A. Dog goes on an hour long walk.

B. Dog comes home physically exhausted, flops down on his bed, and sleeps.

C. He is reinforced by getting to rest when he is tired.

Physical exercise is usually a pretty good predictor for calmness. Here is another predictor for calm behavior:

A. Dog goes to training class.

B. Dog comes home mentally exhausted, flops down on the floor, and sleeps.

C. He is reinforced by getting to rest when he is tired.

It takes a lot less to tire a dog out mentally than it does to tire a dog out physically. I have found that 15 minutes of intense free shaping has as much of a calming effect on a dog as an hour of exercise. You still need to exercise your dog, both for his health and as an investment in your relationship with him, but when it is 10 degrees outside, pitch black, and there are 18 inches of icy snow in your back yard, it is much easier to put your feet up in the living room and free shape some fun tricks.

One more common ABC for calm behaviors:

A. Dog follows you all day as you putter around the house and yard.

B. Periodically during the day, he lies down quietly while you go about your business.

C. He is reinforced by getting to lie down when he feels like it.

Now, you can and should take your dog for more walks, train him more, and hang out with him more during the day, but that is only half the story. The other half lies in the consequences in each of these three examples. How could you change the consequences to ensure that you get more of those behaviors you like?

If you are like most other people, your life is hectic. You are probably just relieved when your dog is not bothering you or doing something awful. You would never dream of going over to the couch where your dog is lying down quietly and giving him a treat or affection. For Pete's sake, he might wake up and start bothering you again!

It is understandable if you feel this way, but you are missing a golden opportunity for shaping your dog into a companion you can live with. If you want a dog that is quiet and polite in the house, you have to reinforce that. Every dog calms down sometimes, even if it is only for ten seconds. Find that ten seconds and reinforce it. Go over to Fluffy and cuddle with him. Tell him what a good boy he is for being so quiet. Lying quietly in a corner is not the default behavior of most Pigs Fly dogs. You have to reinforce the heck out of lying down quietly if you want to see more of it. By reinforc-ing the quiet behavior, you can grow those ten seconds of calmness into hours of calmness. If, on the other hand, you don't reinforce the dog for lying down quietly and then yell at/strike/shove him when he is being a nuisance, you have done nothing to increase the quiet behavior and have fed the "annoying" behavior by giving it attention.

Don't let sleeping dogs lie! Make sure that you give your dog lots of gentle affection and attention when he is being calm and not pestering you.

For Wild Behaviors:

A. Dog is home alone or in crate all day and owner comes home exhausted and not in the mood to do anything with the dog.

B. Dog is an unmanageable nuisance that night.

C. Dog gets frequently scolded for being a pest (hey, at least she is paying attention to me!).

As Oscar Wilde wisely observed, "The only thing worse than being talked about is not being talked about." Your dog agrees with this whole-heartedly. He would much rather have you paying attention to him, even if it is in a negative way, than be totally ignored. You may think that scolding him or otherwise "punishing" him is going to make him stop being a nuisance, but it will not. He is looking for attention and you are giving it to him. You are actually reinforcing the annoying behavior.

I do not expect you to be interested in training your dog or to spend time exercising him every night of your life. This is the real world. There will be times when you have other things to do, or are so tired that it is just not possible to do right by your dog. Remember, if you can't train, manage. If you know you will be working late, you know your dog will be extra hyper because he has been cooped up all day. Make sure you have lots of do-it-yourself activities for him to amuse himself with and tire him out. Some suggestions are:

Dogs need mental exercise as much as physical exercise. This Bullmastiff is enjoying figuring out how to get the food out of the buster cube. This could keep her busy for a while…long enough for you to change out of your work clothes and get dinner started.

1. Give your dog a Buster cube or similar interactive toy. This is a round or square hard plastic cube that you put dry treats into. The dog has to figure out how to turn the toy so that the treats fall out. You can either give this to him outside or in a smooth plastic crate with no bedding in it. If you give it to him outside of his crate, he may mark up your walls with it as he pushes it to find out how to get the food out.

2. Tracking in your back yard. Hide portions of food around your yard. You can even do a little trail of kibble from one pile to another. Your dog will spend a lot of time searching them out, especially after he gets hip to the idea of the game.

These are mental games that will very quickly tire your dog out. In addition, you could give him something to chew on—might not challenge him mentally as much, but chewing has an overall calming effect on dogs. Some suggestions:

1. Try out a stuffed frozen Kong or similar toy. It's a good idea to always have a few ready in the freezer for when you want to buy yourself some quiet time. Stuff them with peanut butter, wet dog food, yogurt, cream cheese or whatever else you like. You can also put bits of dog biscuits or any other treats in with the soft stuff so your dog has some variety and challenge.

2. Toss him a frozen marrow bone.

3. Give your dog a bully stick or similar suitable natural chew object. Caution: rawhide and similar natural chew objects are not for strong chewers. They present a serious choking hazard for larger/stronger dogs.

4. Test out the everlasting Treat Ball ™—hollow toy with "everlasting" edible caps on both ends that take quite a while for even the most aggressive chewers to get through.

By knowing when your dog is likely to be obnoxious, you can cut the behavior off at the pass before it starts by giving him an alternative activity. Warning! Do not wait until your dog is acting obnoxiously and then give him a toy or chew item to placate him. Give him the activity before he starts up with his nonsense. If you give him the fun activity after he has become annoying, you will be reinforcing the annoying behavior. Learn your dog's antecedents for pesky behavior and stay a step ahead of the game. God gave you the big primate brain. Use it to your advantage!

A. Phone rings and owner answers it.

B. Dog takes off on a mission of destruction around the house.

C. Dog gets away with it for a while before owner notices, and then owner drops the phone and runs over to reprimand the dog.

Whoo-hoo! Double whammy reinforcer! Every time that phone rings, the dog knows you will be preoccupied and there is a window where he can get in all those "bad" behaviors that you thought you got rid of through punishment (they were only suppressed, waiting for the opportunity to re-surface when the threat of punishment was absent). What's even better, is that his bad behavior gets you off of the phone and gets you to pay attention to him. Score!

There is a whole class of antecedents that roughly mean "owner preoccupied, nothing fun going to happen for dog." Being on the phone, sitting at the computer, and reading a book are all examples of this class of antecedents. It is super easy to predict if your dog will misbehave given this type of antecedent, so plan things accordingly. Think of what you would like your dog to be doing while you are on the phone/on the computer/in the bathroom and train or manage that. Here are some good alternate scenarios:

A. Phone rings and owner answers it.

B. Owner asks the party on the other end to hold on for a second, and sends dog to crate.

C. Dog gets a big treat for going into his crate (or maybe even a chew item to keep him relaxed and quiet) and owner gets to have a normal conversation.

You may think it is weird and inconvenient to always have to ask someone to hold on for a second while you put your dog in his crate, but it is a lot more inconvenient to interrupt someone in mid-sentence while you dash off to yell at your dog and pull him out of whatever mischief he has gotten himself into.

A. Owner sits down to work on computer.

B. Dog positions himself on his bed which is next to the computer.

Success! Now you can get some work done.

C. Owner feeds dog little treats periodically (I sometimes keep a cup of kibble on my desk for this purpose) or praises/pats dog periodically, or gives dog a chew item so that both owner and dog have a nice project to work on at the same time.

It is darn hard to train your dog while you are in the shower, so management is the key in that case:

A. Owner is going to take a shower.

B. Owner puts dog in crate where he will not get into mischief.

C. Owner takes a relaxing shower and knows that his couch will still be in one piece when he gets finished.

Can you see how, like running water, you will be shaping your dog to be calm around the house? Between training reinforcing calm behaviors, training alternate behaviors, and managing when you can't train, you would be surprised at how effectively even the wildest dog can be transformed into a model citizen around the house. As you can see, it does not take any more effort to do things this way than the way you are doing them now, but it does take a little thought and planning. Although it may seem difficult at first, predicting your dog's behavior around the house and meeting it with appropriate action (reinforce, train, or manage) will become second nature and you will not have to think about it.

But, This is My Job!
Barking

Ahh, barking. People hate it so much, and many Pigs Fly dogs bark a lot. Why does your dog bark so much? Probably because he was bred to.

Smaller terriers were used to go down holes after small game. They were selectively bred to bark loudly and a lot once they found their quarry. Their lives depended on it. The purpose of the barking was so that they could be located, even many feet underground and dug out if necessary. A dog that did not bark might find himself stuck underground without any hope of rescue. As you can imagine, the gene pool for small terriers favors barking—a dog that won't bark underground may not be around to reproduce much. Not only does the gene pool favor barking, but also barking at very low arousal threshold. Something as small as swirling leaves outside can raise a ruckus when small terriers are around.

Many hounds also have a low threshold of barking arousal. Barking or baying is the way that the hounds in a pack communicate to each other about who is on the trail and who is not, who is actively scenting and who is not, and the location of the quarry. The sound a pack of hounds makes is almost deafening.

My point in telling you this is that there is nothing wrong with your dog if he barks a lot. Many wild canids do not bark at all, and the ones that do bark, don't bark nearly as much as domestic dogs do. We bred barking into our dogs because it was useful to us. Now that we live in townhouses, we don't like it. You can train your dog to bark less, but let's understand that, from your dog's point of view, he is making a valuable contribution to the household when he barks. We bred that into him.

Only you can decide when and how much barking is acceptable to you. It is a fact that a barking dog is one of the best crime deterrents there is. When the barking crosses the line to public nuisance, you need to change the situation. Think about where and when you want your dog to bark, and where and when you do not want him to bark, and make an ABC plan based on that. I will give you a common barking scenario that is annoying to everyone.

A. Owner on phone or computer, engrossed and ignoring dog. Dog standing next to owner.

B. Within 30 seconds, dog barks.

C. Owner shushes the dog and/or tries to punish the dog.

Yup. You just reinforced the barking by paying attention to it. Here is an alternative:

A. Owner on phone or computer. Dog standing next to owner.

B. Dog remains silent for 10 seconds.

C. Owner pats dog.

Because you paid attention to the antecedents of your dogs barking, you know he will bark when you are on the computer. You know that he will bark within 30 seconds, so you have to reinforce the quiet behavior before that 30 second mark. You can work your way up to longer and longer periods of quietness using the same schedules of reinforcement as you used to teach stays and attention walking. If your dog barks, steel yourself and ignore it. If the barking is too intense to handle, leave the room and leave your dog closed in the room alone for a little while. He will quickly learn that "quietness" is the behavior that gets him the attention he is looking for.

Here is another one:

A. Dog is in crate in another room.

B. After an hour, dog barks.

C. Owner runs in and yells at him (Thank God! I'm not isolated anymore!).

Dogs crave social interaction almost above anything else. It is hard to imagine something worse for a dog than being isolated from the rest of the family. When you run in that room, you end the dog's isolation, and that is his primary concern. The fact that you yelled at him is secondary. His barking made you appear, and he will bark again.

Here is how you work away from barking:

A. Dog is in crate in another room.

B. Dog does not bark for five minutes.

C. Owner returns to dog and praises him/give him treats.

Just like the lying down quietly next to you while you are on the computer behavior, you can gradually expand that five minutes of silence to hours of silence. If you don't feel like going in every five minutes to reinforce, give your dog something to do, like chew a bone or toy that will keep him quiet. Train if you can, and if you can't train, manage.

You know your ABCs now—whatever your dog's barking problem, you know how to solve it.

Piggy Pointer

If you have a dog that barks when you are not home, the best thing you can do is leave plenty of activities for him to do. Kong has come out with an ingenious, automated Kong dispenser called KongTime™. You can load it with several treat-filled Kongs and one will be released every few hours during the day. Many people have found that this device alone is enough to end their dog's barking and destructive behaviors while their owners are out of the house. Kong bills it as "doggy daycare in a box" and the reviews I have read seem to bear this claim out.

Dog Projects
Chewing

Dogs need to chew and they need to chew a lot. Pigs Fly dogs do not have "soft" mouths like a retriever, and they tend to destroy everything they chew. Dogs are foragers by nature and, left to their own devices, would spend much of the day chewing on all kinds of edible and not so edible stuff. Because dogs like to chew so much, chewing can be both a problem and a solution—a problem if they are chewing something you don't want them to, but a handy management and reinforcement tool if the dog is given an appropriate object to chew.

Two behaviors cannot occupy the same place at the same time. If your dog is busy chewing something appropriate, she can't be chewing something he shouldn't be chewing. (photo courtesy Clean Run)

Chewing is a very calming activity for dogs and also a constructive way to re-direct "mouthy" type behaviors, like nipping and grabbing clothing. If you want to buy fifteen minutes of peace with a young and rambunctious dog, a nice bully stick will settle him down like magic. All in all, chewing is a great behavior, so long as your dog is chewing something he is supposed to be chewing.

First, figure out when he is likely to be chewing something he is not supposed to be chewing, manage those situations, and then give him plenty of opportunities to chew things he is supposed to be chewing. Here is a classic chewing scenario:

A. Owner sitting down to balance checkbook.

B. Dog lies under table and chews on chair rung.

C. Dog enjoys the crunching sensation of the wood as the rung slowly dwindles to the diameter of a toothpick.

Do you see a pattern, here? Any time you are going to be involved in a very engrossing task, your dog may do something you don't like, unless you give him a project to work on, put him in his crate, or you are able to train him by reinforcing him for quiet behavior at the same time that you work on your engrossing task (not always easy).

Some suggestions:

A. Owner sitting down to balance checkbook.

B. Dog lies under table.

C. Dog gets a nice stuffed Kong to chew.

Or:

A. Owner sitting down to balance checkbook.

B. Dog goes to mat.

C. Owner periodically gives treats to dog and praises/pats dog for staying on mat.

General suggestions for controlling chewing:

The key to ending chewing problems lies mostly in management. Pick up your shoes. Don't leave your underwear in a laundry basket on the floor. Whatever it is, if he will chew it, put it away. Don't leave a young dog alone in a room with a veritable smorgasbord of upholstered and wooden furniture.

Make sure there is always an ample supply of "legal" chew toys. I don't mean one rope toy in the whole house. I mean that, wherever that dog is in the house when the fancy strikes him to chew, there is a legal chew toy in plain view. You can mail order very inexpensive rope toys by the dozen and have them in every room. You should also have baskets of toys around the house so your dog knows where to find a toy if he needs one. If your dog is a strong chewer you should always have many Nylabone chews and toys available and your dog should always have at least one in his crate with him.

If you make a mistake, and your dog does wind up chewing something that you do not want him to chew, take it away from him without (outward) emotion, and give him an appropriate chew object.

Have structured chewing sessions. Dogs aren't determined to chew things to tick you off—if they have ample opportunity to chew appropriate objects, they will leave the other stuff alone. Make it a point to send your dog over to his mat and give him a great thing to chew a couple of times a day. Like other "problem" behaviors, when we give our dogs opportunities to indulge in chewing at our convenience, they will tend not to chew when we do not want them to.

Run Faster, Push Harder!
Charging Through Doors

Dogs charge through doors because they want to get to the other side. If you make staying on the same side more reinforcing than charging the door, your dog will stay on the same side.

Here is what you probably have now:

A. You put your hand on the doorknob.

B. Your dog quickly inserts himself between you and the door and presses his nose to the door.

C. Despite your best goalie maneuvers, about fifty percent of the time your dog manages to blast past you through the door.

How about this, instead?

A. You put your hand on the doorknob.

B. Your dog backs away from the door and stays there.

C. You go through the door, toss him a treat, and close the door after you.

Ruby is excited to go outside and runs to the door, but she has learned to back away from the door and sit politely until I open the door, go through, and release her. For added safety, I have trained her to sit automatically on the other side of the door and wait to be released again.

Here is how you can teach it:

1. Start by asking him to back up when you put your hand on the doorknob and treat him for that.

2. Once you have the back-up, you can ask him to stay and reinforce that while you open the door a crack.

3. Open the door an inch and treat your dog for staying in place, then two inches, then three, and so forth.

4. Finally, step through the door and throw a whole bunch of food down for your dog as you close the door.

Isn't it a pain in the rear to have a dog that sticks his head in the fridge every time you open it? Despite your repeatedly informing him that the fridge is not a self-service snack bar, you see the following sequence again and again:

A. You open the refrigerator door.

B. Dog sticks his head in and steals something.

C. You chase him and wrest what is left of it out of his mouth as you give him what-for for having stolen the food.

Nice try on the punishment. Those mouthfuls of your best cooking that he managed to toss back before you caught up with him are awfully reinforcing. What do you think he learned from your punishment once you caught up with him? He learned that next time he should run faster after he steals the roast.

How about using that back up you trained, instead?

A. You open the refrigerator door.

B. Your dog automatically backs up.

C. You toss him a tidbit from the fridge.

Ask him to back up every time you put your hand on the door handle, and then promptly reinforce that behavior. He will eventually back up automatically when you open the fridge.

Gotta Go

Housetraining Issues

Given the opportunity, dogs housetrain themselves. They have a strong instinct not to dirty their den. Puppies as little as three weeks old will make an effort to relieve themselves away from their den area. So long as they have the chance to go outside when they need to, they will housetrain themselves as soon as they are physically able.

Sometimes, though, it seems as if your dog is just not getting the hang of being housetrained. There are many different reasons why your dog might be soiling in the house. If your dog was previously housetrained and is suddenly having accidents in the house, a physical problem should be the first thing you suspect. There are all kinds of sicknesses that can lead to incontinence, and your veterinarian will know what tests to run to diagnose a physical problem or rule it out. Often a round of antibiotics is all that is needed to cure incontinence.

If your dog is under a year old and he occasionally just goes in the house without warning, understand that is natural. Like young children, some dogs develop physical control over their bladder and bowels faster than others. It appears to me that dogs under a year sometimes don't even feel the urge to go and are surprised to find themselves dirtying the house. Some dogs will be perfectly housetrained at eight weeks, and some dogs will be unreliable until they are a year old. Although it is not desirable to have a dog that still occasionally messes in the house at 10 months old, there is not necessarily anything wrong with that dog.

If your dog is over a year old, you have ruled out any physical problems, and he is still going in the house, chances are he is not getting enough opportunity to go when he needs to.

Dogs have such a strong instinct to go outside their den (or house) to relieve themselves that housetraining is somewhat self-reinforcing. Because of that, this section focuses mostly on the antecedents. If you can nail those and get your dog out the door when he has to go, housetraining is a snap.

To crack a tough housetraining case, the first thing you need to do is keep a scientific record of when your dog goes. Note when and where he went, what activity he was doing prior to going, and what physical signs he gave just before he went. You will be surprised at how predictable your dog's bathroom habits are. Here is a breakdown of the kinds of antecedents you will discover if you pay attention to your dog.

Length of Time. The first important antecedent that you will glean from this research is a specific length of time; you will learn that the passing of a certain amount of time, be it fifteen minutes, two hours, or ten hours, predicts your dog's need to relieve himself. Whatever that length of time is, make sure you take him out before it has elapsed. You may think that you are taking your dog out "all the time" but when you start keeping records you might be surprised to find that you are not as reliable or as routine as you think you are. If you are not home during the day to take him out, have a dog walker come in.

The most common housetraining problem I see is that people have unrealistic expectations of how long a puppy can wait between trips outside. A young puppy may need to go out fifteen times a day. A two year old rescue dog that has never been housetrained also might need to go out fifteen times a day. The more predictable you are about taking out your dog when he needs it, the more likely he is to "hold it" until you let him outside. Every time you give your dog the chance to go outside when he needs to, he is reinforced by being able to honor his instinct to be clean. Every time you fail to get your dog out in time and he goes in the house, you have damaged your dog's instinct to go outside and he is reinforced for going in the house by the relief he feels. Remember the definition of reinforcement? Reinforcement increases behavior. Thus, every time you get your dog or puppy outside in time, you increase the behavior or going outside. Every time you fail to get him out in time you increase the behavior of soiling in the house. Eventually, you will not need to go out so many times a day, but with puppies or remedial dogs you need to take them out often until the behavior of going to the bathroom outside is a strong one.

Time of Day. The second antecedent that you should look for is a certain time of day. For instance, say this is your usual ABC:

A. Owner leaves for work at 8 AM and returns at 6 PM to let dog out.

B. Dog goes outside.

C. Dog is reinforced by being able to go outside and keep his den clean.

Your adult dog will probably not have any trouble holding it for those ten hours. However, if one day you changed your ABC to this:

A. Owner stays home until 2 PM, lets dog out, and then does not return until 10 PM.

B. Dog gets the urge around 6 PM and by 9 PM cannot hold it any longer and goes in the house.

C. Dog is reinforced for going in the house because he got relief from extreme discomfort.

Your dog will have a great deal of difficulty holding it, even though it is for the same length of time. Try this, instead:

A. Owner stays home until 2 PM, lets dog out, and then does not return until 10 PM.

B. Neighbor comes in to walk the dog at 6 PM, his usual time to relieve himself.

C. Dog is reinforced by relieving himself outside.

Pay attention to any patterns—if your dog is consistently having accidents at the same time each day, make sure he gets taken out just before that time.

Activities. If your dog has done any of the following:

1. Woken up from a nap

2. Eaten dinner

3. Drank water

4. Played

5. Had something very exciting happen to him

It is a safe bet that you need to take him outside. Pay attention and take note of how long after these activities you dog needs to relieve himself, and make sure you take him out before that length of time has elapsed. Withhold food and water for a few hours before bedtime so that he has a better chance of making it through the night. Make it easy for him!

Doggy Signs. This is where you get to pretend that you are a scientist in the bush, studying the habits of the wily and elusive "Dogus Familyus." Devote some time to observing your dog and you will see that he always gives you a "tell" when he is about to go. If your dog is one of the ones that goes to the door and scratches or barks, this part should be easy. However, it is not always that clear. Young puppies or dogs without a good history of being let out when they asked will sometimes go to the door without barking or otherwise indicating that they need to go out. They might stand there for a while, waiting for you to notice them. Just as likely, they will make a quick pass at the door and, seeing it closed, will go off in a corner and relieve themselves.

Dogs will often sniff before they go, but sometimes they may just barely peck their head to the ground. They may walk differently, or abruptly cease whatever activity they were doing and start walking pointedly towards a corner, they may circle or any other number of things. Your mission is to observe your dog and learn his signs, then run to get him out the door as soon as you see one.

If you pay attention to these four things—how often your dog needs to go, what time of day he needs to go, what activities predict that he will need to go, and what subtle signs he gives before he goes, you will be successful in keeping your dog from going in the house. As your dog comes to know that he can rely on you to let him out regularly, he will be willing to hold it for longer and longer periods of time, and he will start moving towards the door in anticipation of being let out when the need arises.

All of the foregoing pertains to ensuring that your dog reinforces himself as often as possible by eliminating outside. You also have to make sure that he does not have the opportunity to reinforce himself by going in the house. If your dog or puppy is not housetrained, you should be watching him every second they are loose in the house. If you can't watch him, put him in a crate. If he is a young puppy or unhousetrained adult dog, keep him in an exercise pen with a designated potty area. Be extra careful not to close your puppy or dog in his crate for longer than he can hold it. If you have taken note of your dog's antecedents to needing to potty, you know about how long he can stay in there. Don't push the envelope too far and make him soil his crate.

At night, put your un-housebroken dog or puppy in an exercise pen with a crate attached to it. Put some papers or wee-wee pads in one corner. When your dog sleeps through the night for four or five nights without using the paper, you can start closing him in the crate at bedtime. If you try to push it and close him in for the night before he can hold it, you run the risk of forcing him to soil his crate.

Another tip that will help you with housetraining your dog is to put elimination on cue. As soon as you see the signs that your dog is about to go, say "Go

You can use your puppy's crate or exercise pen as part of your housetraining efforts.

Potty" and then praise him profusely and give him a treat after he is done. You could mark the behavior with the clicker, but that will cause your dog to interrupt his activity and I think it is better to let him get on with it.

It's Nothing Personal
Aggression

Aggression is such a natural part of a dog's existence that it is virtually impossible for you to go through life with a dog and never see any displays of it, so you do need to take the time to learn about it. How you respond to your dog's aggression can determine the difference between a happy family pet and a dog that needs to be euthanized.

Aggressive displays are a natural and necessary part of a dog's vocabulary. Here, the dog on the right has invaded the other dog's space. The dog on the left is saying, quite appropriately, "Buddy, back off!" A growl and a lifted lip are information—the dog who does these things is not comfortable.

Go to the AKC's *Complete Dog Book* and take a look at the standard for your dog's breed. Does it mention "guardian" or "aloof with strangers" or the like? That means your dog has been selectively bred for centuries, if not millennia, to be mistrustful of and protective against "outsiders." That is his job and he is doing it very nicely. How horrible for him if you "correct" him for behaving so fabulously! It is not his fault if the world has changed and there is no longer a job market for his skills. Likewise, if you read your dog's breed standard and it includes any kind of killing of other animals or fighting with other dogs, (that would be the entire Terrier group and much of the Hound group) don't be flummoxed and ticked off when these traits surface. What you need to do is put these dogs on the unemployment line temporarily and teach them a new set of skills for making a living.

If you are dealing with an aggressive dog, I suggest that you pick up a copy of Pamela S. Dennison's *How to Right a Dog Gone Wrong* and Jean Donaldson's *Mine* (see Resources). Resource guarding is a sub-set of aggression that almost every dog owner has experienced to one degree or another. Examples of resource guarding are a dog who does not like you to put your hand in his food dish, a dog that will not let other people or dogs near you, a dog who growls when you try to move him while he is on the bed, etc. Resource guarding is such an inevitable part of a dog's existence that I think that every breeder and shelter should include a copy of Jean Donaldson's *Mine* with every puppy or dog they place.

There is not room to tackle the full subject of aggression in this book. There are several good books written on dog aggression, and, if you have an aggressive dog, you need to buy them and spend lots of time learning all about aggression and how to handle it. I would, however, like to give you some guidelines for dealing with it.

Let's understand why a dog would engage in aggressive behaviors. The dog is using a behavior that he believes is an appropriate one to ward off that which he fears or feels threatened by. Here is the important point that humans just do not understand: in the world of dogs, aggression is an appropriate response to a threat. Unfortunately for dogs, aggression is not acceptable in this human world that we have dragged dogs into. If you can show your dog that a different behavior (one that you happen to find acceptable) will actually work better than aggression to ward off the scary thing, he will leave off the aggressive displays. If you grab him and scruff shake him and yell, "NOT acceptable," you will probably get a lot of approving nods from people around you, but you will have done absolutely nothing to teach your dog a response to threat that is acceptable to human society. Your dog will certainly aggress again.

Piggy Pointer

Don't be discouraged if you feel offended or angry when you dog displays un-savory behavior. If it is natural for our dogs to do some "horrible" things, it is equally natural for us to get reflexively furious when they do those things. If a dog ever growls at me or destroys something I value greatly, my first impulse is to drop-kick that dog across the room. As attractive and satisfying as that option seems at times, better judgment prevails and I manage, train, or condition, as the case warrants. We are the humans with the big primate brains and opposable thumbs. We can control any situation without force or anger. Not that I don't sometimes think wistfully about whupping my dog's butt, I just control myself.

So, how can you practically deal with aggression? The first rule is, no one gets bitten. That means that you always stay below your dog's threshold of aggression. Do only that which will not provoke your dog. Until you have trained your dog and can call on foundation behaviors to substitute for aggressive behaviors, stay safe and manage so you can avoid conflict. I am going to give you two common aggression situations that can be easily changed using your ABC knowledge. These two examples will help you, but, if you have a seriously aggressive dog then find yourself a good professional trainer to help you out.

Here is the most common aggression situation that dog owners complain about:

A. Dog is on the bed and owner approaches.

B. Dog growls.

C. Owner shoves dog off bed or moves dog aside and gets into bed with the dog.

Remember the first rule of dealing with an aggressive dog? No one gets bitten. This ABC scenario violates that rule big-time. It is a recipe for disaster. The dog's growl is information. The information he is giving you is that he may bite you. It is like someone pointing a gun at you and saying, "Stop, or I'll shoot!" Please heed this warning and be thankful that he gave you a chance to get away without being bitten. You can train away the behavior later—just don't get bitten now!

Here is an even worse one:

A. Dog is on the bed and owner approaches.

B. Dog growls.

C. Owner grabs dog by the sides of his face and shakes him or hangs him up by his collar and chokes him until he stops growling.

Wow. You just punished out your dog's warning system. If you are successful in your punishment your dog will not growl anymore to warn you that he is going to bite you. Next time, he may just bite you "out of nowhere."

Those sound like scary dogs, but in many cases this is an absurdly easy behavior to change. How about this:

A. Dog on bed and owner approaches.

B. Owner calls dog, dog jumps off the bed and sits in front of owner.

C. Dog gets clicked and rewarded.

It is almost comical how often a growling dog can be instantly transformed into an eager training subject, reporting for duty, simply by asking the dog to do something. A human approaching the bed can become a cue for your dog to automatically get off the bed. It really is that simple. Just get over the fact that it is hurtful and scary when your dog growls at you, and ask him to do something that is incompatible with sitting on the bed and guarding it. Don't confront him over this issue, just train an alternate behavior. Ta-da! Your dog will no longer guard the bed and no one gets bitten.

Remember, these scenarios assume that you have trained extremely strong foundation behaviors. If your dog is not yet that well trained, keep your bedroom door closed. If you mess up and your dog gets on the bed, lure him into a safe area with a dish of food and make sure you don't make the mistake of leaving the bedroom door open again.

Here is another common one:

A. Owner walks into a room where two or more of her dogs are hanging out.

B. Dogs begin to fight.

C. Owner yells at them and breaks it up.

If you know your coming into a room predicts a disagreement between your dogs, how about this, instead?

A. Owner walks into a room where two or more of her dogs are hanging out.

B. Dogs run over to her and sit/stay in front of her.

C. Each dog gets praise, attention, and treats so long as they hold their position.

Can you see how simple it is? Strip away the fact that dog aggression is stunningly scary and offensive, and you see that, voila! Aggression is just a behavior and will respond to training like any other behavior.

11

Just Being With You Makes Me Better

Living and Training in Harmony

When you train with the methods in this book, just being with your dog becomes a dialog. You will find that it is incredibly easy to integrate dog training into your life. Once you have taught the basic foundation behaviors, you never need to have a formal training session with your dog again; just being with your dog will shape him into a model citizen.

Life is a Reinforcer
Finding Time to Train Your Dog

You do have the time to train your dog. Whether you realize it or not, you already are spending a lot of time training your dog. Every minute you are with your dog you are training him. Your everyday interactions with him are the most powerful training tools you have.

Your dog depends entirely on you for all of his needs. If he wants to eat, you feed him. If he wants to go outside, you open the door. If he wants to come out of his crate, you let him out. If he wants his toy, you get it out and throw it for him. Everytime your dog wants something, that something can be a reinforcer for something that you want him to do. If you are going to give your dog something he wants or needs, that is an opportunity for you to ask for something in return. Head scratches, belly rubs, play sessions, treats, and walks, are all things that you dispense to your dog and they all represent training opportunities. Since you do all of those things everyday for your dog anyway, you can train your dog without taking anymore time out of your day than you are already giving your dog.

Remember these two concepts:

If you do things for your dog without asking him to do something for you, you have trained him not to work to get what he wants. You have trained him that he is free to ignore you until you signal that you will be gratifying one of his desires.

If you ask him for a behavior in exchange for doing things for him, you have trained him to work for you to get what he wants. You have trained him that he had better pay attention to you because you never know when a reinforcement opportunity might arise.

Anytime your dog wants to go out or come in the house, you have a golden opportunity to train something. He wants something that only you can give him. Why not get a little something from him in return? Ask your dog for a sit before he rushes through the door. You should work on door etiquette, where your dog sits and stays before the open door until you release him.

Meal time is the grand-daddy of all reinforcement opportunities. Do you want to teach your dog to start up the riding tractor and mow the lawn for you? You could probably do it if you used your dog's dinner as a reinforcer—that is how exciting dinner is to most dogs. The sight of that food dish is invested with intrinsic meaning that can turn your dog's eyes into pinwheels. Well, even if you couldn't teach your dog to mow the lawn, you could probably teach him something useful to you. You could tell your dog to "go to your crate" before you feed him dinner. He will probably be so excited that he will tear off to his den and hit it with such force that it ricochets off the wall. You could also put your dog in a sit-stay and slowly lower the food dish to the floor. If he stays, he gets released to the food. If he does not, pick up the dish and try again. You could just put your dog's food dishes on the floor, but that would not be teaching them anything. Do you see how it takes no extra effort to train a useful behavior at mealtime?

These small, daily, relationship building activities are way more valuable than an hour everyday of formal training. They teach your dog that your working relationship is a life partnership and does not begin and end in obedience class. I have only given a few examples of how you can shape your dog to be the dog of your dreams without any formal training sessions. The secret to success is that you have to plan and manage as much of your dog's day as possible. It does not take much time, but it takes thought. Don't be discouraged if you are not immediately transformed into an organized, well planned dog trainer who can effortlessly produce a perfect dog, just by regular daily interaction. You will get there, someday, but start small. If you can just catch your dog doing one right thing, be proud of yourself. You will find it very reinforcing that you can make a big difference with so little effort, and you will catch your dog in the act of doing something right more and more often.

Piggy Pointer

When I say that you can train your dog without formal training sessions, that assumes that you have already spent some time training basic behaviors and a few tricks. Think of those behaviors as tools that you will use in your life with your dog. If you want to build a house, you will need tools and you will have to go to some effort and expense to get them. However, just having the tools is not going to build your house for you. It is what you do with the tools after you have them that counts.

Beyond Dominance Voodoo
The Magic of Training

By now, I hope you are getting a much different picture of your Pigs Fly dog than before you started reading this book. Your willful, lazy, stubborn dog, the one who was deliberately ignoring you when you asked him to do things, is actually none of those things. He is just a normal dog. A normal dog that would love nothing better than to be trained.

But wait, maybe there is hope that you don't need to do all that pesky training—maybe your dog is just dominant! Maybe you just need to show him who's the boss! Couldn't you somehow just project your dominance over your dog and have him magically become a model citizen? Unfortunately no, you can't and for a multitude of reasons. As of the time of the publication of this book, I am not aware of a definitive study on the hierarchy within a dog-human family as a social unit. Dominance theory as we know it was based on some very limited observations of wolf behavior made in the middle of the last century. The findings themselves were suspect and are no longer the standard for the academic study of dogs, or even wolves.

Furthermore, the way that dog trainers have interpreted and applied this "dominance theory" is way off the mark. For instance, if a dog misbehaves, some trainers will advise forcibly rolling a dog onto its back and holding it there as it struggles. This is supposed to be an assertion of dominance over the dog. The original wolf study concluded that the higher ranking wolf was rolling the lower ranking wolf onto its back. Subsequent observations proved this to be untrue—the lower ranking wolf offers its belly as an appeasing gesture. We now know that a wolf would never forcibly roll another wolf onto its back unless he was going to kill the other wolf. Can you imagine the mental damage done to a dog by rolling him on his back and holding him there as he freaks out?

Most trainers no longer use the "alpha roll" as it is called, but many still advocate programs that stress assertion of "dominance" over the dog by making the dog feel uncomfortable, either mentally or physically. An easy-going dog will probably put up with this, but you can easily push a less forgiving or more frightened dog to the point where he will get fed up and bite you. As I said in the section on aggression, the first rule is that no one gets bitten, and anything that puts you and your dog in danger of conflict is an unnecessary and poor training choice for the average pet owner.

The scientific definition of "dominant" is "in control of resources." Dominant animals control access to food, water, and space. When your dog learns how to drive to the grocery store and buy dog food, you can start worrying about who is dominant in your house. Until then, just have fun training your dog and build a relationship based on cooperation instead of conflict.

Aside from the prospect of damaging your dog mentally and perhaps creating real defensive aggression, the overriding problem with dominance theory is that it prescribes voodoo-type rituals to establish, reinforce, or change dominance over the dog or between two dogs, rather than focusing on the actual behavior and taking training steps to change that behavior. By voodoo rituals, I mean things like, "always go through a doorway first" or "always eat your dinner first" or "never allow your dog to win at tug games" and so forth. By all means, you should train your dog to wait at the door until you

It is completely immaterial who goes through the gate first. The important thing is that your dog has been trained to wait politely for direction on either side of the gate.

release him, lie quietly in a down stay while you eat your dinner, and release a toy on cue. Those things, if trained without the use of aversives, will reinforce your position as the giver of all good things and teach your dogs that you control everything, so they need not try to get around you or squabble among themselves for resources. The path to resources is through you, and by doing what you like, not by "beating out" you or another animal in the household. There is nothing inherently educational for the dog if you just jam your way through the door first or actually put food in your mouth before they do because "you can't let them win."

I suspect that people cling to dominance theory like a life raft because they desperately want to believe that there is some way other than training to get their naughty Pigs Fly dogs to act like the nice, biddable ones. There are no magic wands or dances that you can do to transform your dog into a model pet. If you want to eliminate problem behaviors for good and keep you, your dog, and anyone else, no matter how small and weak, safe, you have to know your ABCs and train your dog to behave nicely.

I hope I have coaxed you to let go of thinking of your dog as unintelligent, untrainable, and having a bad attitude. Now you need to let go of thinking of your dog as dominant, too. Well, what is left, then? Just you, your dog, a clicker, and anything in the world you would like to teach him.

Why Bother?
Your Perfect Dog

Billy the Cattle Dog can be running dead out after a squirrel and all it takes is one word for him to snap around like a boomerang and race back towards me. Honestly, sometimes it is so fast I can't actually see him turn—I just see him running away from me and then I see him running back towards me. He will stay with me all day off leash as I ride the tractor around the property and do chores. If I

called one of my Bull Terriers off of a squirrel, they would slow down, look at me, and then they probably would come back to me, but there is a possibility that they would trot over to where the squirrel escaped and bark at it. I would never trust my Bull Terriers off leash except in protected areas—as well trained as they are, they are only 99 percent compliant, and that 1 percent of non-compliance could get them killed. I always have to be managing them in order to keep them safe.

I have seen herding breed dogs that will stay in a car, unattended, with all the windows open, and never dream of jumping out until given permission. Not only would I never leave my Bull Terriers in a car with the windows wide open, leaving them loose in the car at all is an assumption of risk. At all costs, I will crate my Bull Terriers when in the car. I know of one person who left her Bull Terrier loose in a car while she took a short run into the store. When she came back, the steering wheel was gone.

There are so many breeds that are relatively easy to keep. They obey commands because they are just waiting for you to give them direction: they don't fight with each other, they are naturally calm around the house, and they get into bed with you and lie politely at your feet. They don't scramble on top of you in the middle of the night, inflicting bruises and sprains in a desperate bid to get closer to you than the laws of physics will allow. They make you look really smart in front of other people because they fawn on your every move. They can be trusted off leash, they can be trained to fetch your slippers without eating a portion of them on the way. They don't have to be watched like a hawk and kept under lock and key in order to keep them from hurting themselves or destroying the household, yard, or car. They are good dogs.

Most people are attracted to "good" dogs, but there are those of us who just can't resist the dog who is always ready to cut a caper. Obedience in a dog holds little allure for me—I have so little obedience to authority myself, it would be bizarre if I sought it out in my dogs. A sense of humor and a flair for the ridiculous mean more to my day to day happiness than a dog  who hangs on my wishes. One of my Bull Terriers once took off running through the yard with a six foot long log in her mouth. She charged towards a group of us and hooked the log behind our legs, knocking us one by one to the ground. We were unable to retreat to safety due to the fact that we were laughing so hard that we could barely move. Most people would not find this funny at all but my family still laughs about it twenty-five years later. I have a thirty-seven pound Bull Terrier who's favorite activity in the world is lying on her back in someone's, anyone's,

lap and making grunting noises while you stroke her belly and she licks your arm. That same dog's second favorite activity is uprooting shrubs and small trees many times her size. If she can't get her mouth around the trunk, she will jump up and grab a branch, hang with all four feet off the ground, and still find the wherewithal to tug at it until it comes down. I can relate to that dog.

Maybe people like us are a little crazy. We go out of our way to own a dog that demands a lot of time and effort to train. Couldn't we still get a lot of satisfaction out of a dog that is a little bit easier to live with? Why bother owning and training a dog whose entire mission in life is to smell, uproot, or destroy conceivable object within his reach? Why not go for something a little more biddable?

To answer these questions, think about how you came to own your dog in the first place, and how you feel about him now. When you were mulling over different breeds or types of dog to own, there was that moment when you looked at a dog of your breed and you knew he was speaking to you. Whatever traits he displayed, they delighted you. You got goose bumps when you saw a sighthound unfold and run with a speed and grace you never thought possible. In that silent moment of beauty, you caught your breath and knew that you wanted to share your life with one of these noble creatures. Unfortunately, that speed and grace is not as attractive when your dog has escaped and is running away from you on a morning when you have to leave immediately to drive your three children to school and then commute to your full time job.

The first time you locked eyes with a terrier, he stood up on his toes, wagged his tail, and you heard him say, "Howyadoin'! Let's play!" You loved that. You saw his little antics as hysterical. When he grabbed that ring toy and hung from it as his handler suspended him from the ground, you were in stitches. When he dashed around the yard, back arched, wheeling from side to side as he body-slammed into the fence, you thought he was a riot. His ever present party spirit and no-holds-barred living—that deep appreciation and joy that he can get out of every blade of grass, every patch of dirt, and every person he meets—made him your soul-mate. Now that you own him, you just wish that his ever present party spirit did not include wrecking the entire house, and that his no-holds-barred living stopped short of scrapping with every dog he meets.

My goodness, the first time you laid eyes on your Pomeranian, wasn't he so adorable that it hurt? What a nice little dog, so easy to pick up and carry, so playful. What could be more delightful than a Pomeranian, strutting with all the pride and conviction of a dog many times his size, leaping and scampering while he revels in the pure joy of living. That nice, fluffy coat makes him so cuddly and protects him so nicely in the winter. Yes, you were right, he was cute, but now you realize that he really is a dog, a dog with rather large teeth for his size, and you wish he would scamper a little less—just enough less so you could catch him when you need to, especially when it is 10 degrees below zero, eleven o'clock at night, and you are so cold and tired you can't see straight.

When you visited your local shelter and saw those big, pleading eyes, you could not leave without that dog. Those floppy ears looked so doleful, and that scruffy coat had an adorably rumpled look to it. When you took him out of his cage, he greeted you without hesitation as the special person he had been looking for his entire life. You immediately bonded so strongly with him that you hated to leave him long enough to fill out the paperwork for his adoption. Now that you have had him home for a while your dog is still adorable, but he's also apparently a cross between a Basset Hound and a backhoe. The only time he is not sniffing is when he is digging. Your lawn has so many holes in it that it looks like the face of the moon.

The Pigs Fly dog is generally challenging for the exact reasons that we love him. He is on fire to explore the world. He is often fearless, frequently outgoing, and always ready to have a good time. His powers of reasoning are formidable and rarely at rest. Nothing has changed since the day you picked out your dog—your sighthound is still thrilling to watch, your terrier is still vivacious and entertaining, your plucky toy dog is still an adorable companion, and your mixed breed is still your soul mate. Despite the looks of pity you may receive from "good" dog owners, despite the implied or overt suggestion that your life would just be so much lovelier if you got a nice, quiet, obedient dog, you were right to pick out the dog you did. Whatever he is, he is the dog for you.

Why do we bother with these Pigs Fly dogs? Because we love them, that's why.

Not everyone measures accomplishment in the same way or finds happiness in the same places. I have shown quite a bit in agility with four Bull Terriers and a Cattle Dog. We have gotten lots of titles and blue ribbons, but the biggest moment for me, hands down, was the first time I took Cherry to a fun match (which is not judged and does not "count" for anything) and she actually stayed in the ring and completed the course. I was so happy I was in tears. Being a team with the dog that I loved was the ultimate prize and that prize is within reach of every single person reading this book. Cherry would never have been able to run faster than a Border Collie in agility. However, that in no way diminished the fact that, every single time I stepped up to the line with her, I was sure I was about to run the Best Dog In The World and have the pleasure of taking her home with me at the end of the day.

If you wanted a dog of an "easy" breed, you would have gotten one. You wanted your dog, and you got him. What I have given you in this book is a way to make your fabulous dog a dog that wants to work for you, as well. You can have a sighthound that comes immediately when called, a terrier that listens to you, or a toy dog that plays by the rules. You can have a dog that embodies all of the sublime and ridiculous qualities that you love, that make your heart skip a beat or laugh until you cry, and you can have him be a well trained, good companion, as well…When Pigs Fly.

Resources

Suggested Reading

Note: All my reading recommendations are available from Dogwise at www.dog-wise.com.

Foundation Books Everyone Should Read:

Turid Rugaas. *On Talking Terms with Dogs: Calming Signals*, 2nd Edition. Dogwise Publishing, 2006. Book or DVD. If you own a dog you need to get the book and the video and review them many times. Many of the problems between dogs and people arise from just plain lack of understanding of a dog's body language. You owe it to yourself and your dog to read this book and see the video. It is worth the price of the video to see a big, rambunctious dog calming down before your eyes, just by the owner offering some calming signals he understands.

Pam Reid. *Excel-erated Learning*. James and Kenneth Publishing, 1996. Fantastic and very easy to read, this book delivers on its promise of being an explanation of how dogs learn and how best to teach them. Ms. Reid has taken the daunting and jargon-filled discipline of learning theory and presented it in a clear and concise fashion that you will enjoy reading.

Jean Donaldson. *Mine! A Guide to Resource Guarding in Dogs*. San Francisco SPCA, 2002. This book deals with how to prevent, counter-condition, and train away resource guarding. The preventive section is the best information on this subject I have seen—very clear and easy to follow. I put this in the "must read" section because about 50% of the problems that people ask me about could have been prevented if people had just followed the protocol in this book!

Practical Training Books

Karen Pryor. *Clicker Magic*. Sunshine Books, 1997. Video with small booklet—a really nice illustration of how to clicker train. Most impressive are the recalcitrant mule being clicker trained before your eyes to go into a wash stall and the cat trained to do an agility course.

Pamela Dennison. *Complete Idiot's Guide to Positive Dog Training*. Pearson Education, 2005. A great practical guide to training your pet dog, written in a non-technical style that is easy to follow. Also has the distinction of featuring several pictures of my dogs Nicky and Cherry.

Marian and Bob Bailey. "The ABC's of Behavior" in *The Dog Trainer's Resource*. Dogwise Publishing, 2006. A concise explanation of antecedents, behaviors, and consequences and how they relate to dog training and understanding behavior.

Leslie Nelson. *Really Reliable Recall* DVD. Dogwise Publishing, 2006. Easy to follow steps to train your dog to come when it really counts, in any situation using positive training menthods.

Morgan Spector. *Clicker Training For Obedience*. Sunshine Books, 1998. Although this is a competition obedience book, the entire first section is dedicated to what Morgan calls "fluencies"—essentially what a pet owner would want from his dog, without the precision of competition obedience. Also, the teaching plans and schedules of reinforcement that Morgan gives for the various behaviors are wonderful.

Amanda Book and Cheryl Smith. *Right on Target*. Dogwise Publishing, 2006. Filled with fun targeting and touching behaviors, well illustrated with very complete instructions.

Fascinating Dog Behavior Books

Patricia McConnell. *The Other End of the Leash*. Ballantine Books, 2002. Ms. McConnell is not only a primate and canine behaviorist, but an incredible writer, as well. Her stories are entertaining as well as instructive. Even though I have had dogs my whole life, I saw my relationship with them in a different light after reading this book.

Jean Donaldson. *Culture Clash*. James and Kenneth Publishing, 2005. An insightful and profound book about how dogs think, how dogs learn, and how we can effectively communicate with them. Like Patricia McConnell's book, it is well written and very interesting to read. This is not a dry dog training book!

Stanley Coren. *How to Speak Dog*. Fireside Books, 2002. Immensely helpful in understanding how to communicate with a dog, and how dogs of different type/breeds communicate with each other. I will give a caveat that I do not recommend all the training advice Mr. Coren prescribes, but the book is very interesting, informative, and worth reading.

Brenda Aloff. *Canine Body Language, a Photographic Guide*. Distributed by Dogwise Publishing, 2006. An extremely clear and detailed collection of photos with annotations explaining exactly what each dog's body language is saying. This is a fascinating read and will open your eyes to a whole new world!

Aggression

Pamela Dennison. *How To Right a Dog Gone Wrong*. Alpine Publishing, 2005. Ms. Dennison outlines a practical program for re-conditioning an aggressive dog with positive training, counter-conditioning, and desensitization. I heartily suggest that anyone with a dog with any aggression issues buy this book.

Jean Donaldson. *Mine!* A Guide to Resource Guarding in Dogs. San Francisco SPCA, 2002. See comments in the "Foundation Books" section.

Websites for Training Information and Supplies

American Kennel Club
www.akc.org
Source for information on purebred dogs and dog sports.

Association of Pet Dog Trainers
www.apdt.com

Clean Run
www.cleanrun.com
Source for training toys, particularly the Tug-N-Treat and the Everlasting Treat Ball.

Clicker Solutions
www.clickersolutions.com
Wonderful clicker training site with excellent resources and a chat list.

Dogwise
www.dogwise.com
The source for all of your dog book and DVD needs.

Karen Pryor's Clicker Training.Com
www.clickertraining.com
Very extensive information about how to clicker train.

Lupine Dog Collars
www.lupinepet.com
Makers of great martingale collars. Guaranteed for life, even if chewed!

My website
Madcap Bull Terriers
www.madcapbullterriers.com

Positive Motivation Dog Training
www.positivedogs.com
Lots of articles and information on positive reinforcement training from Pam Dennison.

Doggone Safe
www.doggonesafe.com
Fantastic site dedicated to dog bite prevention. They offer games and other inter-active materials that will help you and your children learn how to safely interact with dogs.

Soft Touch Concepts
www.softtouchconcepts.com
Makers of front hook harnesses.

Stacy's Wag'N'Train
www.wagntrain.com
Very good site on learning theory, training, and behavior.

Pet Edge
www.petedge.com
Source for inexpensive rope toys and other chew items.

Reinforcement Schedules

For most basic pet obedience behaviors, it is best to reinforce (with food, praise or any other reinforcer) every repetition of a behavior you desire. Everytime your dog sits, lies down, or comes to you, he gets a treat, a pat, or a warm word of praise. There are some behaviors, however, that you cannot train this way. If you want to train a behavior that goes on for a long time, such as a stay, you can't reinforce each second of the stay, or you will never get anywhere. Similarly, some behaviors are actually a series of behaviors repeated again and again. Walking on a leash is a good example of this. If you reinforced every single step of walking, your dog would only ever learn to take one step.

You should use a variable reinforcement schedule when you are teaching dura-tion behaviors, such as stay or walking on a leash. With a variable reinforcement schedule, you give your dog reinforcements in a way that are both systematic and random. Systematic, because you steadily increase the time or repetitions between reinforcements. Random, because you increase that interval between reinforce-ments in such a way as your dog cannot predict when the reinforcement is coming. For example, let's say your dog can walk for five steps with you. You take five steps as an average (mean), and work around it, sometimes reinforcing two steps, sometimes three, sometimes seven, and so forth. Once your dog is doing that very well, you can move on to a mean of seven steps, then a mean of ten steps, and so on. Your dog is learning to do the behavior for longer and longer periods of time, but it does not feel that way to him. He maintains interest, yet still winds up giving your more and more of the behavior between treats. You can use this system to teach behaviors like stay, as well. Instead of steps, you would measure seconds

Why do the reinforcements have to be random? Why can't you just reinforce every three steps, then four, then five and so forth? If your dog knows that he gets a treat every seven steps, he will lag, sniff, or pull for the first six steps, and then present himself for the treat at the seventh step. Also, if you are always making it harder in a predictable fashion—today you do two steps for a treat, tomorrow three steps, and the day after four steps—your dog will figure it out very quickly. He will perform the behavior right around the time you are going to reinforce him and ignore you for the rest of the time.

It is difficult to think up a variable reinforcement schedule on the fly, so I have given you some samples, below. You can use the exact schedules, or make up your own variations. I recommend that you make little crib sheets with the reinforcement schedule you plan to use that day and carry it with you during your training session. No matter how hard we try, we humans tend to be very predictable in our reinforcement patterns, and randomness is the key in this process. Although these schedules talk about steps, they are equally applicable to seconds, as in seconds of a stay. Thanks to Morgan Spector for allowing me to reprint these from his book, *Clicker Training For Obedience*. Sunshine Books, 1998.

Example for dog walking with you:

Level 1 (mean = 5 steps): 5 steps, 2, 6, 3, 7, 3, 5, 1, 7, 4, 3, 5, 1 (52 steps total)

Level 2 (7 steps): 7 steps, 3, 10, 5, 8, 4, 7, 2, 5, 10, 3, 7, 2 (73 steps)

Level 3 (10 steps): 10 steps, 5, 8, 4, 12, 6, 10, 3, 7, 10, 5, 12, 1, 10, 3 (106 steps)

Level 4 (12 steps): 12, 6, 10, 4, 15, 7, 12, 6, 15, 8, 12, 2, 10, 4 (123 steps)

Level 5 (15 steps): 15, 7, 12, 8, 13, 6, 20, 2, 10, 7, 15, 9, 20, 12, 8, 15, 7, 3 (189 steps)

Level 6 (20 steps): 20, 10, 12, 8, 15, 9, 17, 10, 25, 15, 3, 20, 10, 25, 13, 5 (217 steps)

Level 7 (25 steps): 15, 25, 12, 20, 5, 15, 25, 2, 18, 30, 12, 25, 15, 20, 25, 12, 3 (279 steps)

Level 8 (30 steps): 25, 30, 15, 20, 10, 17, 35, 5, 25, 30, 15, 20, 35, 17, 30, 15, 5 (349 steps)

Acknowledgments

Thanks to Pam Dennison for being my best in-person training buddy and obedience coach, for getting me started with positive training, and for believing that my dogs were no different than other dogs and could perform just as well as Golden Retrievers. I am not sure that a couple of my dogs would even be alive, never mind winning blue ribbons in agility and obedience, if it were not for Pam. Most of all, thank you, Pam, for encouraging me and showing me how to have confidence in one's abilities and reach for the brass ring. Thank you also to Pam's dog, Beau, who, although he is a Border Collie, was so challenging to train that he earned an honorary position in the Pigs Fly hall of fame.

Thanks to Terri Bright for being my constant virtual training buddy. I can honestly say that Terri helped me develop, think about, and refine every single concept in this book. It is so rare to find a friend who matches one's enthusiasm (OK, obsession) for a topic, and is a great human being to boot—I am very lucky to have Terri as a friend. Thanks also to Terri's dog, Fanny, the Red Rocket. If Fanny had not thought that busting out of the agility ring and running off with a section of ring fencing around her neck was a fine idea, I am not sure Terri would have become such a great trainer.

Thanks to Louie Ruediger for taking the photos that made this book come alive. His vision, design sense, and patience with his subjects are awe-inspiring. I cannot believe my good fortune that Louie agreed to do these photos! Thanks also to his dog, Ace, for not being easy to train so that Louie was interested in this project.

Thanks also to the following people: Kathy Riley, for free shaping Nicky to go around a cone and totally changing the way I thought about dog training. Mary Remer, for being patient and generous enough to share the wisdom of her decades as a breeder and trainer, and for always finding the time to take my "panic" calls. Victoria Corse, for selling me my first crazy Bull Terriers. Erica and Fozzie, for continually reminding me by word and deed what girl power can accomplish. Line Farr, for sharing her vast knowledge of dog training and providing every scientific angle of a training problem. Brenda Buja, for being probably the best dog trainer in the world. Jacky Satch and Bookends, for graciously helping me put together the proposal for this book and pitching it for me. Magda Omansky, Mike Ciarella, and the Norwiches for your encouragement and friendship. Erin Schaefer-Philbert, for showing me how to make the pigs fly. My parents, for raising me to believe that love of animals is a basic human virtue. All of the dogs and people on Positively Bull Terriers and Team Bull Terrier—your tales of woe and subsequent progress through the years are part of the inspiration for this book. I love every one of you!

Thanks also to the models who donated their time for this book: Sandy Baker and and her Pug, Gabby, Alida Cantois and her Leonberger, LCA Ch. Jamaica Vonalpense (Cheyenne), Bridget Davis and her Vizsla, Ch. Garnet-Thaar's Royal Flush CGC, TDI (Andy), Cindy DelSignore and her Labrador Retriever, Princess Knotika of Camelott (Knotika), Erica Eatchason and her Newfoundlands, Rocky Harbour Fozzie Bear RL1, TN-N, NAP, NJP (Fozzie), and Rocky Harbour Surprise Engagement, (Molly), Line Farr and her Phaoh Hound, Ch. Val-Ed's Majic Nikita Avalonn CGC (Kody), Claire Gelok and her Rhodesian Ridgebacks, DC Spring Valley's Half Diamond, MC, NA, FCh, CGC, TDI, HIC, ET, VCX (Mr. Bailey) and Ch. Spring Valley's Pelé, JC, TD, HIC (Pelé), Tracy and Bill Huges and their Chow mix, Dreyfus, the Iacobellis family and their Vizsla, Ch. Braznrock Caveat Shuda Ben'A Cowboy, CGC, TDI (Riggs), Lisa Judge and her Australian Shephard, Jessie, Lynn Keefe and her Bichon, Lily, Andrea Kelly and her Bull Mastiffs, Ch. Bastion's Banshee Riverdance RN, R-1 (Darcy), and Bastion's The Beep Goes On, R-1 (Beep), Bill Larkin and Muttley, Maria O'Boyle and her Basset Hound, Gertie, CGC, and her Terrier mix, Pearly, Magda Omansky, Mike Ciarella, and their Norwich Terriers, Ketka's Biskit OA, OAJ, OAP, OJP, CDC (Biskit), Ketka's Magic Flute NAJ NJP CGC (Magic), and Ch. Littlefield Razz's Matazz at Dignpop (Tazzi), Monica Percival, Anna Jonsson, and their Staffordshire Bull Terrier, Quicksilver Cecilia Snapdragon, OA, OAJ, AD (CeCe), Al and Betty Peters and their Bull Terrier, Madcap Good Life of Corsaire (Riley), Karen Peters-Krüm and her Beagle, Kelli, Julie Swarner and her Golden Retriever, Sassafras Swarner, (Sassy), Maureen Thomas and her Norwich Terrier, Nash Bubba Bridges (Nash), Diane Zdrowski and her Cavalier King Charles Spaniel, Evanlake Fire, Fire, Fire,CGC, TDI (Fiera), and my own Bull Terriers, Corsaire Madcap Cherrybomb, AX, AXJ, CGC, NJC, NAC, (Cherry), Corsaire Night Train, VA, NAP, RL2, CGC, TT, (Nicky), Ch. Corsaire Carpediem of Madcap, VA, NAP, NJP, NAC, RL2, CGC, TT, (Ruby), and Madcap Veni Vidi Vici (Augie).

Last but not least, thank you Charlene, Larry, and Nate Woodward and the entire Dogwise crew. Writing a book, especially a first book, is never easy, and I don't know how I would have done it without your excellent feedback and advice. Your passion for dogs and publishing are evident in everything you do, and it is a pleasure to have worked on this project with you!

Author Biography

Jane Killion got started in dog training when her former husband signed up for an obedience class with their new Bull Terrier puppy, Nicky, and then got bored with it after two sessions. Jane took over Nicky's training and was faced with a seemingly insurmountable challenge—he was so wild that he would literally collapse from excitement when taken out in public. Jane was determined that he should be able to go out and enjoy life like a "normal" dog, so she spent the next several years learning everything she could about dogs, dog behavior, and learning theory. In the process, Jane became a die-hard dog training junkie. Her efforts paid off and she took Nicky on to earn several agility and obedience titles.

Her passion is helping people who have been told that their dog "just has an attitude" or is incapable of learning. She has had great success showing people how to find a new connection with their canine companions by shaping new behavior. Most of all, she never trains for mere compliance—she teaches her students how to shape a dog who vibrates with happiness when training.

Jane lives in New Jersey with a houseful of Bull Terriers and a very wise cat. She breeds and shows Bull Terriers and has successfully competed with five different Bull Terriers and a Cattle Dog in agility and obedience. She has contributed several dog training articles to various publications and magazines. Her house is the frequent site of "Bullypalooza" days, which involve lots of people getting together with their dogs to train all day and then staying into the evening for dinner and lively discussions about dogs and dog training. Her website is www.madcapbull-terriers.com

Index

From Dogwise Publishing, www.dogwise.com, 1-800-776-2665

BEHAVIOR & TRAINING

ABC's of Behav'r Shaping; Fundamentals of Trainingg; Proactive Behav'r Mgmt, DVD. Ted Turner

Aggression In Dogs: Practical Mgmt, Prevention & Behaviour Modification. Brenda Aloff

Am I Safe? DVD. Sarah Kalnajs

Behavior Problems in Dogs, 3rd ed. William Campbell

Brenda Aloff's Fundamentals: Foundation Training for Every Dog, DVD. Brenda Aloff

Bringing Light to Shadow. A Dog Trainer's Diary. Pam Dennison

Canine Body Language. A Photographic Gd to the Native Language of Dogs. Brenda Aloff

Clicked Retriever. Lana Mitchell

Dog Behavior Problems: The Counselor's Handbook. William Campbel

Dog Friendly Gardens, Garden Friendly Dogs. Cheryl Smith

Dog Language, An Encyclopedia of Canine Behavior. Roger Abrantes

Evolution of Canine Social Behavior, 2nd ed. Roger Abrantes

Give Them a Scalpel and They Will Dissect a Kiss, DVD. Ian Dunbar

Guide To Professional Dog Walking And Home Boarding. Dianne Eibner

Language of Dogs, DVD. Sarah Kalnajs

Mastering Variable Surface Tracking, Component Tracking (2 bk set). Ed Presnall

My Dog Pulls. What Do I Do? Turid Rugaas

New Knowledge of Dog Behavior (reprint). Clarence Pfaffenberger

On Talking Terms with Dogs: Calming Signals, 2nd edition. Turid Rugaas

On Talking Terms with Dogs: What Your Dog Tells You, DVD. Turid Rugaas

Positive Perspectives: Love Your Dog, Train Your Dog. Pat Miller

Predation and Family Dogs, DVD. Jean Donaldson

Really Reliable Recall. Train Your Dog to Come When Called, DVD. Leslie Nelson

Right on Target. Taking Dog Training to a New Level. Mandy Book & Cheryl Smith

Stress in Dogs. Martina Scholz & Clarissa von Reinhardt

The Dog Trainer's Resource: The APDT Chronicle of the Dog Collection. Mychelle Blake (*ed*)

Therapy Dogs: Training Your Dog To Reach Others. Kathy Diamond Davis

Training Dogs, A Manual (reprint). Konrad Most

Training the Disaster Search Dog. Shirley Hammond

Try Tracking: The Puppy Tracking Primer. Carolyn Krause
Visiting the Dog Park, Having Fun, and Staying Safe. Cheryl S. Smith
When Pigs Fly. Train Your Impossible Dog. Jane Killion
Winning Team. A Guidebook for Junior Showmanship. Gail Haynes
Working Dogs (reprint). Elliot Humphrey & Lucien Warner

HEALTH & ANATOMY, SHOWING
An Eye for a Dog. Illustrated Guide to Judging Purebred Dogs. Robert Cole
Annie On Dogs! Ann Rogers Clark
Canine Cineradiography DVD. Rachel Page Elliott
Canine Massage: A Complete Reference Manual.
Jean-Pierre Hourdebaigt
Canine Terminology (reprint). Harold Spira
Dog In Action (reprint). Macdowell Lyon
Dogsteps DVD. Rachel Page Elliott
Performance Dog Nutrition: Optimize Performance With Nutrition.
Jocelynn Jacobs
Puppy Intensive Care: A Breeder's Guide To Care Of Newborn Puppies. Myra
Savant Harris
Raw Dog Food: Make It Easy for You and Your Dog. Carina MacDonald
Raw Meaty Bones. Tom Lonsdale
Shock to the System. The Facts About Animal Vaccination...
Catherine O'Driscoll
The History and Management of the Mastiff. Elizabeth Baxter & Pat Hoffman
Work Wonders. Feed Your Dog Raw Meaty Bones. Tom Lonsdale
Whelping Healthy Puppies, DVD. Sylvia Smart

Dogwise.com is your complete source for dog books on the web!

2,000+ titles, fast shipping, and excellent customer service.

| Welcome | Featured Titles | Shows & Info | Publishing | Bargain Books | Help/Contact |

Browse Dogwise

Search Dogwise

Everything

GO

Books & Products
* By Subject
* Dogwise Picks
* Best Sellers
* Best New Titles

Book Reviews
* Find Out How

Resources & Info
* Dogwise Forums
* Dogwise Newsletters
* Dogwise Email List
* Customer Reading Lists
* Dog Show Schedule
* Let Us Know About Your Book or DVD
* Become an Affiliate
* APDT, CPDT
* IAABC
* CAPPDT

Help & Contacts
* About Us
* Contact Us
* Shipping Policy

Employee Picks!
See which books the Dogwise staff members love to read.
* Click Here!

Dog Show Supplies from The 3C's
* Visit the 3c's Website
* View our selection of 3c products.

Save up to 80% on Bargain Books! Click here for Sale, Clearance and hard to find Out of Print titles!
* Click Here!

Prefer to order by phone? Call Us!
1-800-776-2665
8AM - 4PM M-F Pacific Time

Featured New Titles

STRESS IN DOGS - LEARN HOW DOGS SHOW STRESS AND WHAT YOU CAN DO TO HELP, by Martina Scholz & Clarissa von Reinhardt
Item: DTB909
Is stress causing your dog's behavior problems? Research shows that as with humans, many behavioral problems in dogs are stress-related. Learn how to recognize when your dog is stressed, what factors cause stress in dogs, and strategies you can utilize in training and in your daily life with your dog to reduce stress.
Price: $14.95 more information...
DIG IN

SUCCESS IS IN THE PROOFING - A GUIDE FOR CREATIVE AND EFFECTIVE TRAINING, by Debby Quigley & Judy Ramsey
Item: DTO230
The success is indeed in the proofing! Proofing is an essential part of training, but one that is often overlooked or not worked on enough. We all know the story of the dog who can perform a variety of behaviors perfectly in the backyard but falls apart in the obedience ring. This book is full of great ideas and strategies to help your dog do his best no matter what the distractions or conditions may be. Whether competing in Rally or Obedience, trainers everywhere will find this very portable and user friendly book an indispensable addition to their tool box.
Price: $19.95 more information...
DIG IN

REALLY RELIABLE RECALL DVD, by Leslie Nelson
Item: DTB810P
From well-known trainer Leslie Nelson! Easy to follow steps to train your dog to come when it really counts, in an emergency. Extra chapters for difficult to train breeds and training class instructors.
Price: $29.95 more information...
DIG IN

THE DOG TRAINERS RESOURCE - APDT CHRONICLE OF THE DOG COLLECTION, by Mychelle Blake, Editor
Item: DTB880
The modern professional dog trainer needs to develop expertise in a wide variety of fields: learning theory, training techniques, classroom strategies, marketing, community relations, and business development and management. This collection of articles from APDT's Chronicle of the Dog will prove a valuable resource for trainers and would-be trainers.
Price: $24.95 more information...
DIG IN

SHAPING SUCCESS - THE EDUCATION OF AN UNLIKELY CHAMPION, by Susan Garrett
Item: DTA260
Written by one of the world's best dog trainers, *Shaping Success* gives an excellent explanation of the theory behind animal learning as Susan Garrett trains a high-energy Border Collie puppy to be an agility champion. Buzzy's story both entertains and demonstrates how to apply some of the most up-to-date dog training methods in the real world. Clicker training!
Price: $24.95 more information...
DIG IN

FOR THE LOVE OF A DOG - UNDERSTANDING EMOTION IN YOU AND YOUR BEST FRIEND, by Patricia McConnell
Item: DTB890
Sure to be another bestseller, Trish McConnell's latest book takes a look at canine emotions and body language. Like all her books, this one is written in a way that the average dog owner can follow but brings the latest scientific information that trainers and dog enthusiasts can use.
Price: $24.95 more information...
DIG IN

HELP FOR YOUR FEARFUL DOG: A STEP-BY-STEP GUIDE TO HELPING YOUR DOG CONQUER HIS FEARS, by Nicole Wilde
Item: DTB878
From popular author and trainer Nicole Wilde! A comprehensive guide to the treatment of canine anxiety, fears, and phobias. Chock full of photographs and illustrations and written in a down-to-earth, humorous style.
Price: $24.95 more information...
DIG IN

FAMILY FRIENDLY DOG TRAINING - A SIX WEEK PROGRAM FOR YOU AND YOUR DOG, by Patricia McConnell & Aimee Moore
Item: DTB917
A six-week program to get people and dogs off on the right paw! Includes trouble-shooting tips for what to do when your dog doesn't respond as expected. This is a book that many trainers will want their students to read.
Price: $11.95 more information...
DIG IN

THE LANGUAGE OF DOGS - UNDERSTANDING CANINE BODY LANGUAGE AND OTHER COMMUNICATION SIGNALS DVD SET, by Sarah Kalnajs
Item: DTB875P
Features a presentation and extensive footage of a variety of breeds showing hundreds of examples of canine behavior and body language. Perfect for dog owners or anyone who handles dogs or encounters them regularly while on the job.
Price: $39.95 more information...
DIG IN